For many children growing up in the 1950's era.Little money,recovery from the recent war and a time of limited opportunities.

My memories of the time are from a childhood growing up in the south of England where the war had been on the doorstep,subsequently evidence of it was all around and still survived well past my school days.

From conversations it is apparent that what I experienced was closely mirrored by many children growing up at the same time in far flung areas of England.

I hope that the random snapshots of my life can invoke memories in the readers of their own experiences and enable them to recall their own adventures and stories.

Memories are random thoughts and the text is written for that reason in the same way.Pick it up, read any page and you will be with me in an adventure as it took place all those years ago.

^^

As autumn drifted into winter, October mists and grass sodden with dew were replaced with cold frosty mornings and impending fog, which was fuelled by the smoke of numerous chimneys. Bonfire night had burnt its way into the past once more and winter clothes, scarves, balaclavas and gloves had come out of mothballs, along with sturdy winter shoes which were pressed into service once more.

In the half term before the fifth of November I had been to Clarks shoe shop in the High Street with Nana and this year I had been bought a new pair of shiny, black lace-up shoes. I didn' t have many pairs of new shoes bought for me, they were expensive and very often they were worn till they were too small, they pinched my toes and water began to enter through the holes in the soles, even lined with cardboard the water still filtered in.

This day, before they could be worn, it was necessary to visit the cobbler in Whitworth Road and to make a purchase of four shiny, metal, kidney shaped protectors, which had several metal nails set in them, enabling them to be fixed onto the toes and heels of the new leather soled shoes. Grandad would place the shoes on a cobbler's last, nearly every home had one, and hammer the plates in place, I loved them as you could slide better on the paving stones.

On the route home, we had on this day made a detour to a little shop which was a delight to behold, a fair cornucopia of exciting trinkets as well as more mundane treasures.

++

Earlier that morning, stood on the doorstep in Leesland Road, I had watched a neighbour from opposite, as he and his wife made their way down the road.Every morning at the same time they would walk slowly down the road to open their shop next to The Junction Public House in Whitworth Road and this was where we had now arrived.The tall stooped gentleman,dressed in a black suit,his long white beard stained yellow from the pipe he smoked,would walk purposefully,supported with a stick,his shorter grey haired wife clutching his arm,acknowledging our greeting,"morning Mr Clogg", by raising his stick in the air.

 The shop was dimly lit,in fact quite gloomy,on the pavement outside was an assortment of various articles,tin baths,galvanised buckets,a simple lawn mower,even a stack of witches besom brooms for sweeping the garden lawn of its worm castes.As we advanced through the doorway we were greeted with a heap of metal dustpans,tin shovels,garden forks,spades and the indispensable,replacement wooden handles.These handles repaired brooms,mops,every kind of garden tool,hoes,prongs,spades and everything else that had a broken grip,repair was cheaper than replacement and the items were like 'good friends",not to be deserted in their hour of need.Inside,the shop was ill lit and full of dark nooks and crannies,a passageway ran down the right hand side,the wall covered in little wooden trays containing all manner of items,to the left a long counter made up of lots of drawers,behind which a now bespectacled Mr Clogg awaited his customers,his wife nowhere to be seen.Each little drawer held its own treasures,each shelf on the wall behind him its own little gem.Tools were to be found everywhere,saws,chisels hammers,axes,screwdrivers,little oil cans,kilner jars,preserving pots and saucepans.Labels and wax paper tops for jam jars,elastic bands,flat irons,a barrel of paraffin oil,putty with the aroma of linseed oil.In the drawers were loose nails and screws,various hooks,chains,candles,washers,door latches and the item we had come to buy,a roll of chicken wire lay on the floor.The shop was as jumbled as this list,but everything had its place,what it sold had no limits,sometimes it was just one of an item,stocked just in case somebody needed it one day. Hardware shops and ironmongers like

this was the salt of the earth and always relied on to have the unheard of,or "impossible to find".

++

It's Sunday morning and on opening the kitchen cupboards there was no bread,no eggs ,no prunes,no bananas,not even a rasher of bacon,but it doesn't matter,we can go to the convenience store,open all day,everyday,but it wasn't always that way.
  As we got into the car and drove to the local village at seven thirty in the morning,I passed others hurrying to make their purchases,before returning home to wait for the supermarket,that sold everything,but specialised in nothing, to open its doors at ten o'clock.
  The church bells were silent,two elderly ladies were going through the church lych gate and up the gravel path to the heavy oak church doors to join the few figures already inside.On returning home I began to remember how it had been when I was a schoolboy how different it was from the 1950's when I was growing up.
  My first thought was the peal of church bells and throngs of people making their way to church,all impeccably dressed in their Sunday best,well polished shoes,pressed suits and smart dresses.The shops recognised the day of rest,their doors remained closed if you weren't organised then you went without.Your larder had enough food to last and a little extra,and it was a little,in case unexpected visitors arrived..One stop shopping had arguably now reduced the freshness of the food we were eating,it was just fresh because of the additives and preservatives pumped into it.In my childhood you would have had to visit a lot of small shops,all experts in their chosen field,there were

bakers,butchers,dairymen,fishmongers,greengrocers,florist and grocers.They all readily imparted their expertise when asked and you could purchase in the quantity you needed,as opposed to what you had to buy ready packaged,so we bought only what we deemed to be needed.

Bananas were a treat,vegetables seasonal,fish when available,cheese limited in variety,but the changes at the grocers was

probably where you would see the biggest change,apart from the opening hours.Most opened Monday to Friday nine till five thirty with an hour for lunch, one o'clock till two.Saturday and Wednesday were half days so only opened nine till one,and Sunday,nobody opened.

I could run down to Mr and Mrs Hornes,on the corner of Leesland Road and Norman Road and be enthralled,the various smells accompanying the purchases.Vinegar could be bought in a jug,dispensed from a wooden barrel,ham on a china stand would be carved by hand,bacon rashers would be sliced from a side of bacon,green or smoked,using a large hand operated red bacon slicer.Fray Bentos Corned Beef, Chopped Pork or Luncheon Meat would be removed from large tins then sliced on a slicer which varied the thickness of the slice.Sugar would be weighed from a large sack as would the required amount of prunes,raisins,sultanas and currants,the fruity aroma filling the air.Biscuits in glass topped square tins,either as broken biscuits or individual varieties would be weighed into paper bags.Rice was sold loose,many items you could buy singly,you bought only what you wanted or could afford.

I miss those days,and the atmospheric shopping of the 1950's when the various characters we met were all helping to enrich the whole experience.

++

It was only Sunday,a quiet dreary day and in 1958 still three days before the annual bonfire event.As was usual, waiting for a nine year old boy was not something that came easy,the bonfire was built,the fireworks purchased and the required refreshments for the big day,a Wednesday,were stored safely in the scullery.With one eye on the weather and one on the state of the bonfire as it became damp,thoughts ran to what would happen if the fire never lit.Eventually Sunday drew to a close and apart from viewing other bonfires as I made my way to Leesland School,on Monday morning noting whether they had been reduced in size by clandestine pilfering,there was little to do except wait.

   The weather had been mostly dry in the ensuing days,although a few showers had made the bonfire a little suspect to ignition so a top up of paraffin oil from Mr.Clogg's emporium was on standby..The day seemed to never end,excitement filled the air and arriving home from school I could hardly contain my patience whilst waiting for the adults to arrive home.Many families could be found heading towards HMS St Vincent the training barracks in Forton Road where the Royal Navy provided a superb public display,killing time before their own back garden displays finished the evenings entertainment.Tiers of benches had been erected around the parade ground with its tall mast being the focal point,no health and safety to be seen.No rails to climb up the steep steps,no rail to stop you falling if you were on the top seats of the stands but even more astounding no safety harnesses for the naval cadets manning the mast as a finale to the parade ground display.You held your heart in your mouth as the lads climbed up the mast and out onto the yardarms,the final boy,the button boy,standing at the very top on the smallest circular platform you could ever see.The display fireworks,compared to the ones we were to later set off were huge,green and red rockets sailed into the sky,giant Various Roman candles spewed out golden sparks and acrid smelling smoke pervaded the air,Suitably applauded the crowds mingled amongst themselves as the filed out from the barrack square,occasionally accompanied by squeals of mixed fright and excitement as the odd mischief maker threw a jumping jack amongst the fleeing legs of the crowd. Having hurried home, wrapped warmly in hats, scarfs and gloves to protect from the increasing damp and chill, the bonfire was ready to light crowned with the guy from the shed, The damp wood resisted doggedly until, as if by magic, certainly with scant regard for safety, although with a moderate amount of common sense, Grandad would empty copious quantities of paraffin oil onto the wood and paper. Walking around the pile it was lit in a number of places, as it burnt and the ashes built up, potatoes in their jackets and recently collected chestnuts were placed unwrapped in the glowing embers. Whilst the fire began to settle, mugs of hot tomato soup appeared from Nana's kitchen to warm us inside, the bonfire performing the same task warming our outside. Blackened potatoes, now well cooked were removed from the ashes, cut open and butter added before we gnawed our way through them, "a little ash never harmed anyone" we were told.

Hunger satiated it was now time to watch the fireworks. "Stand back", we were instructed some even watching through the window from indoors, as Grandad scurried back and forth. Catherine wheels flew through the air having escaped their pins, rockets collided with the wall as the milk bottle fell over and Mount Vesuvius and Sparkling Leaves toppled over and provided an unwelcome display to the verdant grass. Grandad, meanwhile thought he was back in World War 1 and spent his time frantically attempting to escape the bombardment, hiding in the shed, all in all it was close to a complete disaster.

At last as the chill, damp air became filled more and more with swirling smoke from the many fires and projectiles, the bonfire was checked to prevent further burning and it was time to retire to bed. The one night a year event was over again, the following morning the milkman on his rounds cursed the soot laden bottles which had launched numerous rockets, the schoolkids searched for and collected the spent rocket sticks. We had fifty days to wait, in my case thirty four, before the next exciting step of growing up would arrive and how different that was in those days.

++

 What a week it had been,inclement weather bringing cold and damp and Saturday the last chance to make the final preparations.If everything wasn't ready by Saturday evening it would be too late.Most of the day was spent rounding up the last scraps of wood in the old blue pushchair and transporting it to the ever growing bonfire in the back garden.At lunchtime however I had to ensure I was outside one of the local public houses, accompanied by the silent guy in the pushchair,this was a propitious time,several over indulged individuals,aided by the alcohol and unable to differentiate the coins in their pockets, would mistakenly impart a half crown or two bob in error,as my cry of "penny for the guy"met their ears..As the premises closed I hurried home to count the spoils and add the new sum to the previous collections.If I had collected too much,that was the adults definition of too much I was persuaded to keep some back for Christmas presents later in the year,it was not right to let all that money"go up in smoke" I was told..The guy was placed in an armchair,where stared fixedly at Grandad until the big day arrived,part of the family.The no longer needed pushchair was returned to its corner of the shed,its eventual demise I can't recall.As evening fell we would make our way down to the newsagents in Whitworth Road to obtain a late copy of the Portsmouth Evening News,printed on pink paper,which gave us the chance to catch up with all the local football scores and allow Dad to check his football coupon.The coupons from Vernons or Littlewoods gave ordinary folk the chance to wager a few pence on a line of football matches,The resulting "homes,wins and draws" scoring points.Eight draws promising a life changing sum of money.However this Saturday evening there was an added task, it was time to buy our fireworks for Guy Fawkes night, the night of November the Fifth.The array of various types of incendiaries was limited,but nonetheless created much anticipated excitement to the queueing purchasers,.Fireworks were mostly purchased singly,although boxes were available,the main manufacturers being,Astra,Brocks and Standard,the items only on sale for a week before the day and never on sale after the fifth.They were only let off on the traditional evening,never before or after,they were nearly all ignited in the limits of small family celebrations,just a small amount of organised displays such as the one at HMS St Vincent existed..

 The fireworks were selected from a display safely locked behind a glass counter,there were Roman Candles,Mount Vesuvius,Penny Bangers,wonderful scary Jumping Jacks,Catherine Wheels,Rockets and Sparklers,Packets of six or twelve sparklers were either small ordinary items or large red or green monsters,all sold in white paper packets.Matchboxes contained matches with large brown heads with green or red tips which when struck flared up in the colour of the tops.Money exhausted we wandered home where Nana or Grandad took the fireworks to the shed,placing them up high out of reach and it was expected that they wouldn't be touched or mentioned until the evenings party began on the appointed day..Nobody let fireworks off on a Sunday,so if Bonfire Night fell on that day it would normally be held on the Monday night,a little longer to anticipate the display that we had purchased for but The Lord's day must be observed.

 I had been aware for some time that languishing in the corner of Nana's shed lay an old pale blue pushchair which had seen better days.It had spent most of its last fourteen years transporting my sister and then me on the journey from Leesland Road to Oxford Road, as well as on other various journeys until the day arrived when it was no longer needed.Its usefulness outgrown it just lay gathering dust,until now,once more. it became an item of usefulness before finally departing forever,so now it was just what I needed.

 Pulling it creakily into the yard I was greeted with "what are you doing with that,I don't want that dirty thing brought indoors".Grudgingly I started to clean it before getting a little can of oil to lubricate the wheels,two hours later having laid newspaper on the floor of home,to catch any oil or remaining grime,I pushed it down the passageway and out of the front door.It was half term,it was October and time was short, in ten days time it would all be over for another year.A couple of pals joined me,so with a "just going out Nana,not going far" we joined forces and pushchair to hand we started to hunt.We made our way down the road to the shops at Lees Lane crossing shops and timidly entered them one by one,some we came out of empty handed but others were more fruitful in our search.As we returned up Harcourt Road we climbed the wall of the cemetery and went around the back alley ways checking every hiding place we could imagine before returning home with whatever we had managed to collect in the way of wood.Once we had manoeuvred the pushchair back through the passageway, into the back yard,we piled up its contents onto an empty patch of soil in the back garden.It was only small,but it was a start and by the end of half term it would be as huge as the garden would safely allow.We had made a start and now it was time for the next step on the way to Guy Fawkes night.

  The next step was to use the pushchair,once more,as a conveyance for an occupant too tired,or unable,to walk.Having eaten dinner I could be found constructing the elderly passenger surrounded by old socks,old trousers,old shirts,old stockings,an old cap,string and the most important item old well read newspapers.Having removed all the buttons from the clothes,to the button tin,we tied string around the legs and sleeves of the old clothes and then proceeded to stuff newspaper into them with the result,once assembled,of it having the semblance of a figure.A circle of cardboard,cut from an old cornflake packet had a face drawn on it and we had a temporary "Guy",hoping that a few days later we would be able to purchase a proper "moulded.painted face mask".from the planned "collections.Suitably tired I went to bed,the anticipated excitement preventing me from falling asleep until I could fight the desire to sleep no longer and drifted off to the land of dreams.

++

The watery sun next morning heralded damp pavements and there was a chill in the air,but nothing was going to prevent today from happening,gulping my breakfast,with most people still preparing to leave for work,I was found grasping a tin in one hand dragging the pushchair,complete with Guy,through the house to the front doorstep.A cardboard sign had been scrawled on a piece of cornflake packet saying "penny for the guy" so it was propped up on the pushchair and I started my wait. Roads were quiet,apart from local residents,only one or two people passed by but they were implored to relinquish a penny or even a halfpenny and most did.Once I had enough to purchase a proper "guy" mask I could run down to the newsagents in Whitworth Road and choose my "face"before returning happily to replace the crude homemade version.

 I would sit outside Mr. Horne's grocery shop on the corner of Norman Road,then as the week continued we made our way to farther locations,sitting outside The Junction or Forester's Arms public houses,often several children's guys vying for their share of the spoils.
 Begging was not acceptable,even for the "men of the road", or tramps, as they were better known, but Guy Fawkes with it's "Remember,remember the fifth of November" nursery rhyme was an exception,although illegal, in most cases a blind eye was conveniently turned..Fireworks were only sold for one week before the actual day,a simple tradition that gave so much pleasure was encompassed in one night of celebrating an historic event that could have changed England forever.

++

As summer was slowly expiring, mists would linger in the mornings,the dampness started to fill the air and the dew would lay heavily on the grassy meadows.The blackberries had disappeared,been replaced by hazelnuts and walnuts which we picked to store and use later in the year then they too vanished,replaced by mushrooms,inedible fungi and toadstools..

At this time of year the evenings became laden with choking yellowy smog which could be seen swirling in the glow of the gas lamps dotting the street.Under one of these lamps I would wait for the number six bus to arrive at the bus stop in Leesland Road at its junction with Norman Road ,a golden glow announced its arrival as it came closer. The "smog" fuelled by the constant sulphur and nitrogen laden smoke pouring from every chimney in the terraced houses,its choking presence a necessity if we were to keep warm.As October moved to a conclusion it was time to harvest the last orchard fruits,most of this consisting of numerous varieties of apples the best known Cox's Orange Pippin,the pips rattling inside signalling they were ripe,alongside them grew Charles Ross,James Grieve,Egremont Russets and Lord Lambourn,all following on from the early rosy red Discovery.To leave them longer risked losing them to birds and insects,any blemished or bruised taken for immediate use,those too damaged discarded for natures uses,The perfect fruit were dried,polished,individually wrapped in newspaper and stored in wooden crates in the cool of the shed to keep for Christmas,a similar fate befalling the Conference pears,which rarely ripened on the tree.
Whilst this was taking place the trees would receive their yearly haircut,need had meant nearly all the residents knew how to prune fruit trees and bushes.On the allotment Grandad would have a pile of green twigs,too small to burn on the home fire,so with a pile of damp leaves we would add to the smoke laden air.With fondness I can see the white whispy smoke from the smouldering bonfire as it rose from the leaves,the smell of the apple wood was delicious.
In the back gardens,nearly everyone had at least one apple tree,the piles of prunings from them were added to the pieces of scrap wood we had been collecting all month as we prepared for the momentous occasion,Bonfire Night.Autumn was well and truly with us,winter not far

behind and the first frosts had arrived even before the clocks had gone back.

++

The balmy summer evenings had almost faded away,the evenings slowly but surely were drawing in and we had already started to prepare for the icy cold winter that almost certainly would soon be with us.Mr Stanley,the log man,with his horse drawn cart, had been delivering logs for several weeks and a couple of hundredweight of coal,every week,from the coal merchant, saw the coal-hole almost filled.As John Keats had written in his "Ode to Autumn" it was "the season of mist and mellow fruitfulness".and for us the opportunity to share some of it with the rest of the population meant a day in the countryside.We would make trips out at the weekend heading to various woodlands and copses,Goodwood being a favourite,maybe stopping at Fairmile Bottom before old wooden Edwardian Cafe closed for the winter,charabanc trips from London to Bognor Regis over for another year.Once in the forest we would gather plump sweet chestnuts,ready to store and be roasted over the open fire at Christmas,we would collect hazelnuts from the coppices,careful not to pick the ones with neat holes drilled through the shell by a marauding grub,picking the glossy brown nuts they separated easily from the little"fairy hats" that held them onto the spindly branches.Nearby the oak would shed its acorns from their "fairy smoking pipes",the beech,not to be outdone littered the ground with mast and seeds.WithIn the hedgerows "robin's pincushions",with fiery red whiskers would adorn the wild dog rose bushes in the same way as the oak apples,minus their little wasps,would appear in the ancient oaks.Gazing at the copper and gold autumnal leaves of the majestic beech trees I often wondered if the little yellow and green packets of Beech Nut chewing gum had any connection.Fallen dry tree branches would be collected and taken home in the car boot to augment the winter's fuel,similarly when they had been collected from the local cemetery they would be dragged slowly along the pavement,all a welcome bonus for the winter fires.At this time of year the first mists used to hover above the furrows of the fallow fields and at Titchfield Haven the deer,as ghostly outlines,grazed on the remnants of the harvested crops,the harvest now gathered in,whilst in the sky skeins of black and white Canada geese flew in to take their share.

As Michaelmas approached,the little purple daisies of the same name became visible in many little gardens,harvest would be celebrated in the parish church,devoid of any sign of the pagan festival of Halloween,or All Souls Day.Such a non christian festival involving the devil was not welcome at a time when if you spill salt you would throw a little over your shoulder"to blind the devil",and throwing even the smallest piece of food in the fire was seen as "feeding the devil".

The seed however which provided the most enjoyment to me,as a little boy,was the horse chestnut,the humble conker which provided hours of fun.At Leesland School or in Green Lane there were lofty trees,which when the winds blew deposited their prickly cases spilling their shiny brown conkers on to the ground.Not quickly enough for me and my friends however,bottles,bricks,shoes,sticks,plim-soles,in fact anything heavy was hurled into the branches to dislodge them,once gathered they would be put in the oven and baked or pickled in vinegar to harden them for combat.Using a meat skewer a hole was made through the nut,also your finger at times,string threaded through and knotted and we were ready for battle.Holding the conker up on the end of its string your opponent would aim at your conker with his,if you moved it they would have a second shot,once taken your turn came next,the aim being to destroy your opponents conker.If you won you would be the proud owner of a "oncer",if the one you had been beaten had already won a "fight" it would be a "twicer" and so it went with "forty niners"and such.Grand days,great fun but just around the corner the fun was going to start with an even bigger BANG!!

++

"Memory Lane" the boxes lay waiting to be opened,the delights inside cried out to be eaten,and whilst indulging the day dream would begin....Memory Lane came in many flavours and led to many places,there was no definitive destination as all the journeys were different as were the cakes in the boxes.Now we have superstores,retail parks and department stores but "Memory Lane is still there to spin the magic albeit in a different guise.All the specialist costermongers have gone but my memory begins outside the front door many years before when with cake in hand I was transported back to the missing links and jobs which we had lost. Mr Shepherd and Mr Stanley. with their horses and carts,gone the horse drawn milk floats,with them the grooms at the stables where they had been quartered.Gone the lamplighter riding his bicycle, turning on the gas lamps with a long hooked wooden pole.no more the figure of Mr Chase,the landlord collecting the weekly rent,nor the gasman emptying overfilled meters.The brown coated baker driving his red electric Co-op bread float,a large wicker basket of loaves slung over his arm as he entered the houses,the muffin man pushing his handcart and the onion "Johnnies" ,not from France but from Belgium,plaits of brown onions hanging from the handlebars of their bicycles.

The rag and bone man collecting recyclable items,the knife sharpener with his handcart sharpening knives,shears and scissors,the Romanies with their wooden pegs were all gone.The coal man carrying his hundred weight sacks on his shoulder,the hawker or tinker peddling his trinkets.I was hardly able to understand how we had lost all these jobs.The hustle and bustle,the friendly banter replaced with a sterile silence.

Crumbs falling down the front of my woollen jumper I walked along a now almost empty road,the little shops which had inhabited every corner had been turned into houses.No dairy.no ironmonger,no butcher,no cobbler at his last.The little wool shop gone as was the

sweet shop,and also the tobacconist.The greengrocer,the baker even the paper shop with its paper boys was disappearing into the past.
 Passing a small builders yard,behind tall wooden gates,the joiner,carpenter and plumber,all skilled tradesmen were being replaced by mechanisation,their skills disappearing.So many jobs,so many skills,so many trades lost for ever,and even in the countryside jobs too were vanishing.No milkmaids on three legged stools or cowherds and herdsman,no pigman,few shepherds,no ditchers,no hedge layers no carters or wagoners in fact very few farm workers.
 At Brickwoods brewery in Portsmouth you could see a cooper making his wooden barrels ably assisted by a blacksmith, who would also shoe the horses for the carter,responsible for the provision of shire horses for the drayman.Even at the end of life the coffin maker and gravedigger had been replaced by mechanisation.Cake eaten, it was time to throw the box away and like these jobs it just became a memory in Memory Lane.

++

 The red sky began to turn pink,as the copper tones of the sun began to disperse the lingering mist lying in the furrows of the fallow brown field.The harvest had been gathered,the stooks stacked in the barns and we had harvest thanksgiving to look forward to.At this time of year all that was left was to prepare for the coming icy blasts and glean what was left of nature's bounty to preserve for the cold winter's days.Saturday morning and it saw me,with Dad walking through the alleyway opposite Oxford Road and turning right up the back of Southcroft Road before following the muddy path round towards Privet Park,Rastus,the golden retriever close behind,we passed the site of the fatal helicopter crash which had occurred a few weeks before,when the stricken craft had crashed into the allotments with no survivors.Entering the park through a gap in the hedge,the mist still lingering over the dewy sward,there in front of us in little white patches was our future breakfast! Why they grew there I know not but those wild mushrooms have never been surpassed in flavour.Returning home,the peeled fungi joined the bacon and eggs in the frying pan,an ample feast to start the day.Breakfast eaten my day was spent at Nana's and at this time of year we saw the delivery of fuel for the winter heating.Mr Stanley with the horse and cart delivered logs,the smell still in my memory of the wood and wicker baskets it was carried in.Mr Blundell, the coal man could carry hundredweight hemp and jute sacks on his back,through the house and empty them in the avaricious mouth of the gaping coal hole.

 Saturday morning was spent making firelighters to store for winter.Made of sheets of newspaper after folding and twisting you arrived at a rigid structure which was long burning but hard to describe.Empty Kellogg's cornflake packets were cut down to the size of a brick and then filled with a mix of cement dust and last years coal dust mixed with water to make a thick gloopy consistency.Left to dry in the last rays of summer,before the weather became too inclement they were stacked in the wooden shed to supplement the coal supply,home made briquettes.

 The weather on the Sunday proved fine so after the weekly visit to the cemetery at Ann's Hill we arrived back home with several small branches to be added to the fuel store.After lunch we would make use of the fine day and head,by car,to Goodwood in West Sussex and a walk up The Trundle,overlooking the horse racing course.

 The copses in that part of the country held a bounty of riches.In the thickets next to the racecourse we would pick cobnuts to be dried in the oven at home.The hedgerow gave up their final crop of blackberries for jam and the mirabelles and wild apples provide a source of fruit to bottle.Sweet chestnuts,after you had collected the spiny green "hedgehogs" eventually they gave up their contents and I dreamed of Christmas.still far away,savoured the thought of roasted delights in the depths of December.

++

As we left St. Faith's church and headed home up Tribe Road, the clouds in the darkening sky stood out against the red fingers of the sun as it gathered in the last moments of daylight.The short journey over, I went and stood in front of the glowing embers of the fire having switched on the little bakelite,battery powered radio and listened to the music furnished by the Light programme.Nana headed to the scullery to warm up the milk for a cup of Horlicks,Ovaltine or Bournville cocoa and she soon was heading back with the drinks and two digestive or butter osborne biscuits to dip in it.

"Drink it up",she said."early bed tonight you've a big day ahead of you tomorrow",

It was now September and this "big day" had been talked about all summer,preparations for it had accelerated in the last weeks and did little to allay my slightly bewildered fears.As I washed and brushed my teeth in the chill of the scullery,I then stood in the front of the fire,pulling on my flannel pyjamas, I could feel the anxiety growing. was I going to be alright,what was going to happen and was I going to be left alone? On the chair next to the bed, the blue enamel candlestick shone its light on a pile of neatly pressed and folded clothes.A white shirt,grey short trousers,string vest and pants,short sleeved woollen jumper,tie,long grey socks and a pair of elastic garters.Next to the fireplace downstairs was a pair of polished black lace up shoes and hanging on the back of the door a black, belted gabardine raincoat,in case it was needed.

I knelt and said my prayers,climbed between the white crisp sheets,pulled up the blanket and eiderdown,then restlessly tossed and turned, fearful as to what tomorrow would bring.Eventually slumber took over and after a fitful night's sleep it was time to rise for that all important day which would set me on the path to whatever would unfold on life's unpredictable journey.

Reluctantly washing and dressing,downstairs I went,breakfast was ready on the table and although hungry I had no appetite and only picked at the cereal and toast put before me.Down from the table I laced up my polished black shoes,a task I had practised all summer,as I had also done with tying my tie.A comb suitably wetted "to get my hair to lay down",a neat side parting put in and a final dressing down with the clothes brush, I picked up my shoe bag and checked the contents,it was all there.

We couldn't afford a leather satchel so the shoe bag contained not only plimsolls, but a little pencil tin with its contents of a pencil,small white rubber emblazoned with the word"Eraser" and a metal pencil sharpener.I was five years old,I was as ready as I could ever be and reluctantly,tightly gripping Nana's hand we ventured out to walk the short journey to school.

Older children confidently scampered happily towards the school gates,interrupted by younger nervous figures clinging to mum or grandma desperately seeking reassurance.As the school gates beckoned the more confident of the new intake entered the playground,whilst a few tearfully clung to their chaperones in the forlorn hope that this experience was just a bad nightmare!!

Through the black painted iron gate and railings, under the shady boughs of the giant horse chestnut trees we traversed the tarmac playground to a big wooden door which was propped open..The established classes were queuing with their teachers at the summoning of the bell,chattering noisily before silence descended and in an orderly fashion.they filed into the vacant classrooms.As we entered into a wide corridor with a wood block floor we were shown into a changing room with benches and coat racks,this was where we hung our bags and having changed out of our outdoor shoes into plimsolls,said our final farewells,accompanied by the odd tear,and proceeded to our classroom.

The classroom had a very high ceiling and was heated by a large open fire,regularly fed with coal from a large bucket which was periodically taken away to be filled by the school caretaker.The windows were high up and being small we were unable to see out,lights on long cables hung down and illuminated the rows of heavy wooden desks on heavy wooden frames.These heavy brown wooden desks had sloping tops which opened to reveal storage for our school items.In the rail at the top was a channel to hold our pencils and wooden handled,nibbed pen and a hole at the end held the ceramic inkwell filled by the ink monitor from a glass bottle of blue ink,Parkers,Stephens or Quink.The iron framed desks had seats that folded up so you could stand up when the teacher entered the room for registration.There were definite signs of past use from the ink stains,clear attempts to engrave ones name and occasional Arrow chewing gum stuck on the underside were a reminder of previous academics.Around the wall were large paper charts,the alphabet,times tables and later the adornment of our very own artistic efforts.One wall was taken up with a huge blackboard,board rubbers,ink bottles,a globe,writing slates,chalks and counting frames stood on various shelves.Here I sat,the future was mine,this was the start,where would it end,where would we go on the way and what would I need to experience before I arrived at my destination?

++

A shy young boy with a nervous smile
A bit of a joker who acted a while
Who made people laugh if you got taken in
By the twinkling eyes and ever present grin.

The thoughtful times when steam ruled the track
The greasy old cap from an engine shed rack
Where it came from I haven't a clue
But it stuck on his head like paper to glue

It seems far more than three score years

That his cheeky wide grin would have us in tears
Our acquaintance was short but my memories remain
Of the jumping on trains in the wind and the rain

That time is gone and now so have you
Leaving us memories of what you would do
Laughter ,compassion knowledge and wit
Dave Rowland your memory is worth every bit!

++

   The last of the sun's rays drained from the August skies and the greyer September evenings heralded the autumnal colours and hues preparing us for the winter ravages ahead.
   The previous week had been busy for all the family,the time to take advantage of the bounty provided by both the wild hedgerows and neatly tended allotments and everyone had their part to play.The raw ingredients,blackberries,wild plums and sloes picked from the miles of hedgerows,apples fallen from the gnarled trees and vegetables harvested from the ever provident allotment now lay piled up to await preserving.
   The Co-operative delivery man had delivered two blocks of salt wrapped in blue and white wax paper embellished with the word"Cerebos", and they were accompanied by little packets of spices,mace,paprika and peppercorns.Packets of preserving sugar,a tin of Colman's mustard powder,white and black pepper and cinnamon sticks joined the whole nutmeg on the table.
   Standing around the scullery there were Kilner preserving jars with glass tops and brass screw tops,alongside jam jars with wax paper discs and paper tops which would be fixed in place with string or secured with elastic bands.Paper labels with a simple glue backing,written in pencil would betray the contents of each jar when

they had been filled to the brim.Already on the table stood bowls,basins,the trusty green "Spong" bean slicer and on the old gas stove large copper and aluminium preserving pans awaited .

 The work now began but not before I had been dispatched to Horne's corner shop for several jugs of vinegar,decanted from wooden barrels

and once home poured into one of the large pots on the kitchen stove.Into the vinegar was added the various spices,wrapped in a little muslin bag and then rapidly boiled before being left to simmer and then put aside to cool.Meanwhile we were all shedding streams of tears as everyone,including me, peeled the pounds of shallots Grandad had pulled from the allotment.Once peeled they were immersed in a large ceramic mixing bowl,or two,of salted water,covered with a clean whitecloth and left to soak overnight.

 Preparation for the pickled onions complete our hands turned to the baskets of runner beans stood on the cool scullery floor.Nana washed them all and then proceeded to "string" them whilst I fixed the green bean slicer on the edge of the table with a large steel screw.Poking the long runner beans in the top,ensuring my fingers were clear of the hand turned cutters the sliced beans piled up whilst Nana crushed the previous mentioned salt blocks with a carving knife and wooden rolling pin.All the salt crushed,the Kilner jars were sterilised with boiling water,dried and cooled before alternate layers of salt and beans were packed into them always finishing off with a layer of salt.The red rubber seal and glass top were placed on the jar,before it was all tightened down with the brass coloured ring lid preserving them till they were required for consumption.

 Whilst all this was taking place one copper pan bubbled away full of sugar and blackberries fast approaching the consistency of the jam or jelly it was to become.Adjacent a pan of apple pieces,cut from the fallen apples,with the remaining berries were stewing down to be put in the preserving jars for pies and suet puddings during the winter.

Evening arrived with preserves and jams everywhere, except there was still a large pan of cooling spiced vinegar standing on the stove.This was to be for the following days task when the brined shallots would be washed,packed tightly into jars,then covered with prepared pickling vinegar to mature.The remaining vinegar would be used to make chutneys from onion,apple,rhubarb and tomatoes and

last of all the piccalilli which was why the mustard powder was there,added to the vinegar,the yellow cauliflower,shallot,and gherkin pickle was my favourite.

++

  August bank holiday 2019,Hot,torrid air,no breezes,crowds rushing headlong to overcrowded litter strewn beaches,overflowing uncollected litter bins,their often obnoxious smells filling the air,Row upon row of air polluting traffic travelling along roads with over cut verges and the carnage of road kill.Kentucky,Mcdonalds,Costa coffee advertised everywhere from litter strewn across roads and pervading into fields and woods all ejected by lazy uncaring occupants of the same polluting vehicles.
  One single man,high in a combine directed by computer,unable to miss the family of partridges on the ground beneath and scattering the leverets,kits,and cubs to find their place in the tragedy of roadkill.
  Hedges of sloe and blackberries devoid of fruit,butchered by the tractors flail as it beat the trees into submission,and beneath it dry ditches.Dry as they were filled with silt or too much water had been extracted,no bulrushes,no crowfoot,no wild watercress,gravel bedded streams reduced to a trickle.Water vole,newts dragonflies they had gone too,with them sticklebacks,minnows and water boatmen.No food for kingfishers,moorhens and rails pacing dry banks with water vegetation non existent.Himalayan Balsam had suffocated the willow

herb along the bank along with purple loosestrife the alien species thrown out by us and destroying the river bank.,

  Swifts and swallows no longer skimmed the water,modern day living deeming their nesting habits to be undesirable and slowly they disappear through progress and unsympathetic development.Soon too they will follow the nightingale,barn owl,finches,bunting,linnets into the annals of endangered species.

  Walking over the fields I was able to hear the sounds of the countryside,they were still there but this time it was the low incessant hum of traffic,the blare of a radio and the incessant drone of a microlight.All this as I walked through the lager cans,plastic bags and abandoned agricultural chemical sacks.

  By now I had fallen asleep and in my memory was quiet roads,people who cared,no litter,small mammals scuttling in water filled ditches.There was fruit in the neatly cut hedgerows,there were wildflowers butterflies and insects everywhere.As you walked across fields grasshoppers would jump in front of you and flocks of small birds encrusted the hedges.Bats were darting in front as you walked at dusk and deer,foxes and badgers could be glimpsed in woodland glades full of flowers.

  Waking up I realised these memories of sixty years ago were now only a dream and prayed that the nightmare of 2079 would be avoided before I fell asleep again.

  This was Gosport, what will it's future be....only we can determine what our grandchildren will experience before it's gone for good and that means every one of us.

++

  The school bell had rung as usual to herald lunch hour at Leesland school and it began a frantic journey,normally at a breakneck pace to get to Nana's,to eat my lunch,then run helter skelter back to school in the space of sixty minutes! The normal jog home took me up Whitworth Road,into Smith Street,cutting through the back alleyways which linked Vernon Close,Vernon Road and Tribe Road before arriving in Leesland Road,outside number 80.This was the plan on this particular lunchtime but it was somewhat disrupted when I reached Vernon Close where unusually there was a large,noisy crowd of people surrounding a large white car.Alighting from the car was a well dressed blonde haired lady who seemed to be commanding significant attention,and appeared to be well known and recognised by the assembled throng.Various comments of "she's ever so famous" and "she's visiting family" could be heard, but to a small boy it meant very little,so pushing my way past I hungrily hurried on to partake of lunch.I arrived at Nana's a little later than normal and she remarked on the fact,so I told her of the pretty blonde lady and she mumbled"oh that'll be ..."but I didn't hear as I had by now washed my hands and was busy eating my food.In contrast to the frantic journey at lunchtime,after school was a more leisurely affair.I walked,well ambled, along the road into Smith Street at the end of which was a yard containing the piggeries.As well as the pigs with their pungent nose invading odour,the yard also housed the Shepherd;s vehicles.Archie was the custodian of the horse and cart used for his vegetable round and his brother Lofty,looked after the large green pantechnicon he used for moving furniture.

 Whilst leaning over the wooden gate of the pig sty,watching the squealing piglets the pigman came out from his nearby house.It was at this point that the cruelty of children,although not meant, but more out of ignorance, became apparent, along with the incongruity of the situation compared with that experienced at lunchtime.

 The young man who tended the porcine animals lived with his mother but everyday whatever the weather he would be out tending his charges,He was tall with black hair and permanently unshaven with black stubble,his teeth yellow with one or two gaps,when he walked it was with an ungainly lurching gait and he was unable to express himself clearly,his speech being bellowing uncoordinated grunts.This was, however due as much to a lack of education as to his unfortunate appearance, he was different and nobody really understood his sorry predicament. His garb of black boots, baggy brown trousers, tied with string, grubby white shirt and an ill fitting brown jacket made up the picture. The children would goad and taunt him, something I now view with regret.

Alan Barnes, as that was his name, was what we now recognise as autistic, then he was just "simple". He was extremely strong and would chase his antagonists with shovels, or even a hand axe, out of sheer frustration, but he was also very gentle and kind and as far as I am aware he wouldn't have hurt a fly. I sometimes wonder what became of him as his mum became older.

The ladies name...I can't recall, but the contrast in circumstances between the two very different people stayed with me forever.

++

Through the long cold winter months, long before we were discussing global warming, when it was icy every morning and our teeth chattered as we walked to school, jumble sales were a permanent fixture. The church hall at St Faith's Church was a regular venue and Saturday afternoons would provide the majority of us with our first experience of womens rugby scrums. As soon as the doors opened, like a plague of locusts, the poor volunteer opening the door was brushed aside and the tea urn standing on a wooden trestle table shook and trembled as the hordes of charging purchasers homed in on the bargains they had spied. The neatly piled garments on the tables soon reminded me of the pile of rags on the rag and bone man's cart, tossed everywhere as people delved for the best items and then held their prizes aloft. The children headed towards the table of toys, many damaged, missing pieces or minus boxes, but to the new, discerning owner the best thing in the world because it was our "new" possession.

Tables of unwanted presents,"useful items",handkerchiefs,eau de cologne,curtains,cushions and all types of household items,another table of books and magazines,and yet another of various footwear,well worn but still serviceable for the poor,but grateful recipients.

But now it was summer time, July,the weather was warmer and the same trestle tables stood in the hall,but some had now spilled outside on to the grassy lawn with their wares as it was the annual Summer Fete,Every parish had one to help raise funds and many items found in the jumble sales now appeared in different guises,added to by various seasonal delights.The tables were now "stalls" displaying their goods,there was a plant stall,book stall,home preserves and pickles,fresh fruit and vegetables,flowers,home made cakes,pies and many more.Tea,scones,fairy cakes and rock buns,homemade lemonade,ice cream soda and even an ice cream cart would provide refreshments.Volunteers from the church congregation manned lucky dips,bran tubs tombolas and luck straw stalls.Hoop la,coconut shies,plate breaking,apple bobbing,pin the tail on the donkey or hoopla all helped to persuade visitors to part with their hard earned cash.Entertained,fed, relieved of most of our spare money we wandered wearily home,chattering about the day,what I had done,how I had almost won the biggest prize and the constant thought of what next year's fete would bring.

++

The warm sunny days with clear blue skies were never ending,only punctuated with odd warm showers and the inevitable thunderstorms when huge "cauliflower clouds" gathered in the distance.Summer holidays were coming to an end and as the August Bank Holiday approached it was a last opportunity for the family to celebrate together before we returned to school.Weeks of fun and games,and some less happy times had been spent doing... well,nothing really,but just having fun.All the family were hoping that the Monday wouldhave fine weather,and afford us the chance to go to Stokes Bay,Apple Dumpling Bridge or any other open space for a final family picnic before autumn set in with its reds,yellows and browns.By the Tuesday morning the realisation that school was less than a week away began to strike home,yesterday was the last holiday until Christmas,next Monday would be the start of the new term.The term that would end with the best time of the year,and only the half term and Guy Fawkes Night to look forward to in between.It was this scenario which greeted us with just six days holiday remaining!What was needed for school in the manner of uniform had already been purchased,or repaired,any "new items" purchased from Harts,the tailors in North Street Gosport,or if there was insufficient money,one of the regular jumble sale at Saint Faith's Church Hall would normally have very serviceable second, or even third hand items for very little money.These jumble sales were always popular and were more akin at times to a scrum or maul at a rugby match at Twickenham than a genteel church fundraising event,as I previously mentioned,Uniforms washed and ironed,shoes polished,football boots liberally covered in Wren's dubbin,name labels sewn in all items,repairs completed,patches applied to knees and elbows where needed and my school bag,or satchel,suitably equipped,so what else was there to do?

At this point in time the ingenuity of children of school age was stretched to its limits,no spare money,unable to go on a day trip so the possibilities were limited....or were they.

If it was inclement weather it was slightly harder but scrap books could be updated from items cut from old magazines,coins would be rubbed,like brass rubbings,using greaseproof paper.The button tin came into its own,along with tiny coloured glass beads which were made into necklaces and bracelets.An old book or box would be covered in cut out pictures of flowers,animals and birds in which to store keepsakes.Little rows of figures holding hands or snowflakes were cut from stiff white paper to make simple fun decorations,old coloured glass bottles had sea shells,collected from the visit to Stoke's Bay earlier in the holidays,stuck to them with plaster then varnished. Then there were the fine days and the great opportunity to play in the garden or street outside either on my own or with neighbouring children..Apart from the usual pastimes,football,cricket,fishing,walking and lounging around talking there were other ways to spend the last few precious moments.We played hide and seek,built dens,we made bows and arrows from no more than sticks and string.We put worms in our pockets and forgot them,until they appeared in the washing basket,we collected car and train numbers,climbed trees,and walls,and mischievously knocked on doors,then ran and hid.

  These appear silly little things,even pathetic,but they cost nothing,hurt nobody,taught me about nature and the environment taught me how to enjoy life and how to spend time happily even with no money,respect and marvel in nature and its bounty it had bestowed on me and how lucky I was.

  Complain,never we didn't have time!

++

  The golden fields were quickly turning to stubble,devoid of the stalks of corn that rippled in the summer breeze as the tractors slowly collected the grain.The sickles and scythes had joined the ancient tractors in the barns and granaries whilst the larger combine harvesters cut swathes through the golden cloaks.Small brick buildings stood on staddlestones in the farmyards.Whilst In the older barns stood the odd redundant steam traction engine from nearly forgotten times,waiting for a collector to buy and return it to its former glory,a distant memory of pre-war farming. August ended and the empty fields stood fallow as the farming year took stock, and ditching and hedging became the labours of the day preparing for winter and next year's harvest which seemed so far away.

It was with these thoughts in my head that I set off down the road from number eighty,dressed smartly as it was Sunday,heading towards the "mission" as Nana called it,but in fact correctly named St.Faith's Church,As we turned into Tribe Road,past the black corrugated tin buildings which housed the dairy delivery carts we espied at the end an Aveling and Porter road roller resting overnight..The green roofed roller, with a giant front steel roller and even taller steel wheels at the rear, had clanked its way around the nearby roads,steered with a mechanism akin to a ships wheel, by a grey boiler suited engineer with

a flat cap,pressing the granite chips into a layer of tar as it travelled.Now as it was the weekend it was parked,covered with a large grey-green tarpaulin,waiting for Monday to resume its duties,safe in the knowledge that it wouldn't be damaged or vandalised.It would have taken too long to go back to the depot,as it was so slow,so parking in a safe location was the best solution, unless it was the only option.Opposite the roller was the entrance,set in a brick wall,to St Faith's Church,the wall continuing to form the boundary to the adjacent Ann's Hill Cemetery.Walking down the path.past the phlox and daisies,in the well kept borders,we entered the building and sat ourselves in a vacant pew,ready to take part in an important day in the Episcopal calendar,Harvest Thanksgiving.Parishioners had spent the previous day,Saturday,readying the nave to receive the abundant produce that the congregation had now carried with them in gratitude for an abundant harvest,the items later given to the more needy in the parish.

 Even in the less rural parishes we took part and were proud of the decorations in our own churches,Beautiful flowers,freshly cut the aforementioned borders and from local allotments,vegetables from the same place and the ever present sheaf of golden corn,a simple loaf of bread made by the local baker,decorated with a red ribbon.The congregation keen to share their wealth with the less fortunate carried cabbages,potatoes,carrots,parsnips,turnips and swede.apples,pears,plums,medlars,quince,jams,pickles and eggs an abundance of generosity.

The service over we would retire to the church hall to partake of a delicious traditional harvest supper,prepared earlier,simple but meaningful,quite often a ploughman's supper of bread,cheese and pickles.Well fed we ventured out to return home,a few small clouds scuttled across the now bright sky,the last few that had dampened the footpath and road with a light shower of rain

As we slowly turned back into the dark of Leesland Road the Harvest moon,brassy.silver,full,shone brightly on the damp road surface,few cars standing in its way,as the moonbeams reflected eerily back into the quiet street.

That wondrous moonlight.....no light pollution from garish street furniture just the simple glow of solitary gas lamps that would allow us to enjoy the riches of the natural light.

++

Stokes Bay has seen many sad times and a fair number of happier times and one of these happier occasions fell on a warm early summer's day in 1953,and one which was replicated again in 1978.People had been arriving in the area for several days and on this particular June day hordes of local people,squadrons of bicycles,pushchairs and prams,all loaded with blankets,coats and hampers of food,crowded every highway that led to the bay.All vying for the best vantage point overlooking the sea at Spithead,once a satisfactory viewpoint was found they settled themselves down to await the culmination of weeks of preparation there to greet their excited gaze was indeed an awesome sight,as far as the eye could see,in the Spithead anchorage was the biggest collection of ships they had ever seen,ships from around the world that had been congregating for several days. There were all manner of warships from aircraft carriers, submarines, destroyers, frigates, mine sweepers and motor torpedo boats to name a few. They were from countries like Pakistan, Australia, Thailand, Italy, France, Germany and Canada, to name a few participating countries, axes had been buried and it reflected the party atmosphere and celebrations as the ale and stout flowed on the crowded beach.

 Merchant ships and auxiliary vessels were in abundance and were carrying all manner of cargoes, coal, oil, bananas, as they headed into

 Southampton Water, even Macfisheries stunning new trawlers made an appearance.

 The crowds waited noisily, variously entertained by aerial displays from squadrons of the RNAS and RAF the review took place on the high sea. The younger children gradually fell asleep, taking a chance to recharge their batteries before the main event then they would need to be wide awake. As dusk began to fall and it became dark lights began to flicker on the ships outlines, the bunting strewn vessels gradually began to spring into life, the outlines illuminated, clear for all to see, until midnight arrived, when darkness reigned once more and the lights went out. As the evening became cooler, a slight breeze blowing on shore from the sea the long awaited firework display commenced, All the children were now wide awake and "oohs and aahs" filled the air as the unheralded sight of so many brightly lit ships and the wreaths of smoke from hundreds of colourful explosions celebrated the coronation of Queen Elizabeth 11. Entertainment over, the weary throng slowly meandered its way back home, quiet pushchairs with their sleeping charges, slightly grizzly tired toddlers, adults merrier than was normal in many cases but all so pleased to see their welcoming beds.

 These memories were some of my first. Later that year we visited Navy Days in Portsmouth Dockyard when access to the ships we had seen was almost unrestricted, visitors encouraged to visit and view what the Navy was all about. The massive workforce to service these ships was enormous,their crews many hundreds and security was little thought about as civilians wandered into even the most intimate areas of our sea defence force.

++

I had looked forward all July to those warm balmy days in the school holidays when we went for an excursion,very often on foot and not always a great distance away.One popular, with the anticipated treats at the end,was Stoke's Bay.It was a favourite destination on the hotter days,it was not too far,an important consideration when carrying food,beach equipment and sometimes weary children.It was such a day that found me and my family,well Nana and my sister,along with other families journeying down Ann's Hill Road,along The Avenue and then Western Avenue to access the shade of Stanley Park.Passing through the park I recall being fascinated by the primitive monkey puzzle tree that grew there and even more so by the Alverbank Cafe with it's ice cream cornets.We must have been a strange site heading towards a day on the pebble beach that overlooked the Solent to the Isle of Wight.Dress code was an incongruous affair,the men dressed in tweed suits,the women in suits with fox fur stoles, all desperately sweating their way to the beach,appearances being all important, Even on arrival at the sun baked beach it would be acceptable dress,very little flesh exposed to the sun,and the bizarre view of men with knotted handkerchiefs protecting their heads still wearing jackets,at least the ladies in their summer dresses had removed their stoles!..
 As the sea came into view ,we held our noses as we passed the smelly stagnant water laced with strands of green algae that was the remains of the old moat fortifications.Crossing the road the rusting sewage outfall pipe with its warning sign came into sight,ideal for mackerel fishing but not suitable for bathing.We headed along the concrete path in the direction of Gilkicker and soon found a reasonable place where we could make our way onto the beach before laying our

travel rug on the pebbles,carefully avoiding the tar which had been washed onto the beach by the incoming tide.

 Suitably settled, we started to unpack,out came the buckets and spades,the inflatable beach balls, kites and an item whose designer,as well as the wearer, must still be having nightmares about,the knitted woollen swimsuit.It was really a strange fashion item,a knitted woollen item in the height of summer and once immersed in water the modesty of any individual,including myself, was instantly compromised,with acute embarrassment.

Dressed appropriately once more,modesty reinstated I would amble further on,passing the remnants of wartime Britain towards the old and fast decaying pier.Stokes bay was never a seaside destination,even Queen Victoria only visited to facilitate her passage to Osborne House,so consequently leisure facilities were very limited.Public conveniences did exist but traditional seaside attractions,fish and chips,candyfloss and such, were conspicuously missing,although a small kiosk did dispense ice creams,and this was to provide the treat we were headed for.The choices seemed endless,in fact they were quite limited,although to a small boy,like myself,a choice of three was a problematic decision.They were mostly provided by Walls or Lyons Maid,you could have a wafer,cornet[not cone] or ice lolly,you could have vanilla,chocolate or strawberry ice cream,orange or strawberry lollies.You might be lucky and have sticky strawberry or chocolate sauce drizzled over the top,and luckier still,some chopped sugary nuts.Strawberry Mivvi,vanilla ice cream on a stick covered in strawberry ice lolly was a real treat but apart from that your choice,at least for a few years, was relatively small.The adults would partake of an ice cream cornet or wafer,either a Walls oblong confection unwrapped from a paper wrapper and pressed into a square cone or sandwiched between two Askeys wafer biscuits.Lyon's Maid cones were slightly different,short stubby cylindrical ices which were peeled from a cardboard wrapper and pushed into short stubby round cones.

If the kiosk was closed it would mean a return walk back to Stanley Park,where we could buy an ice cream cone or have an ice cream treat, sat around a little wooden table on slatted wooden chairs.Heavy glass glasses and dishes with Knickerbocker Glory,Banana Splits and Ice Cream Sundaes,although these were normally reserved for extra special occasions like birthdays.

++

Wednesday afternoon,school holidays and the time when I would,with Nana, make the walk to Alverstoke to visit my uncle, aunt and cousins.The recent shower with its resultant rainbow shining through the water droplets heralded the"brightening up" for the afternoon and over the damp pavements we ventured.A seventy year old lady and eight year old boy must have seemed to be a strange mix of travel companions but when coupled with the distance involved it was not remarkable.
 The matriarch neatly dressed in flowery blouse,neat skirt and sturdy shoes topped with a blue straw hat fixed tightly over a hairnet with a decorative hatpin.The little lad,me,in white shirt,grey flannel short trousers and long grey socks,running along ahead, kicking small stones and trying not to scuff his polished shoes.
 In the front of the little terraced houses,at the lower end of Leesland Road, the small neat front gardens they were lucky enough to have boasted London Pride,Canterbury Bells,Esther Reads and red,pink and white Phlox.The tiny paths of patterned tiles,edged with rope twist earthenware,led to tiny front doors with shining brass fittings opening onto dark interiors.
 As we approached Whitworth Road and The Junction public house,with its hand painted hanging sign displaying its name I would peer inside if the door was open out of curiosity.The long varnished wooden bar of the Brickwood's ale house was lined with a few wooden handled beer pumps,for dispensing the beer,a number of ashtrays and

the odd small towel but little else.Glasses and beer mugs lined the shelf behind the bar,and spittoons stood on the floor which was liberally covered in fresh sawdust to soak up the various fluids which made their way onto it.

 The door slammed shut to prevent my gaze into the the "den of iniquity"as the old lady inside said "go away" and I ran on to explore the other shops in the row.Wednesday afternoon was early closing,a half day of rest for the owners so as they passed the closed doors,peering in the empty windows,I remembered the things I had seen when they had been open,The fish and chip shop,the fryers at the rear and a small marble counter for fresh fish in the window,large glass jars of pickled onions,pickled eggs,aluminium salt pots and glass vinegar shakers standing on a counter shelf next to a pile of old newspapers in which to wrap the fish and chips.

 The hardware shop owned by old Mr Clogg, where when open.you could buy methylated spirits in an old milk bottle,paraffin in a metal jerry can or purchase nails by the pound,weighed out on a small set of scales.Broom heads,broom handles,garden tools,candles,washing line,string,dustbins and any hardware items you could imagine lurked in the recesses of the dark gloomy shop,as well as littering the pavement outside.

 Next door was the post office manned,or womaned by a large lady,probably about forty, in tweed skirt and knitted cardigan,she had an almost comical appearance with glasses,bright red lipstick and a permed post war hairstyle.She happily dispensed postal orders,dog licences,radio licences and envelopes and postcards as well as small stitched books of postage stamps,each page of red,blue,green,violet,brown and orange stamps,valued at a half,one,one and a half,two,two and a half and three pence each,alternately split up with an advertisement page.

 Across the road in a small parade was Shepherds,the local greengrocers on the corner manned by Mrs Shepherd who would perch on a rickety shop stool.The floor was well worn wood,in places so worn it had formed a dip,a large brass potato scale stood on a table and the unwashed vegetables,in season,were in racks around the shop,or in wooden crates and hessian sacks.Muddy root vegetables,misshapen carrots,blemished apples even mud streaked lettuce were for sale,they were all edible they just needed a little effort to wash or trim them.Dyers Dairy was in the same row of shops and its marble counters provided the cold surface on which to stand ceramic milk pails,and loose butter patted to order,as there was no refrigeration.The little shop also sold expensive fresh cream and provided fresh brown and white hen's eggs in various sizes,large,medium,and small and also large blue duck eggs,often with the odd anal deposit or feather still stuck to them!

The butcher's nearby,devoid of meat, betrayed the fresh sawdust floor covering,ready for Thursday morning's business as it spilled out slightly under the ill fitting door onto the pavement.On the marble counter in the window stood large ceramic models of cattle,sheep and pigs.To prevent the sun spoiling the goods and the shops getting too hot,each had sloping blinds which hid from view above the shop windows,Each morning the butcher's apprentice would pull the blind out with a long hooked wooden pole and each evening return it to rest,

 A short distance but so many memories,each day I would arrive at my destination,having learnt so much just by looking and watching,my education being added to at every turn.

++

 Pocket money was never plentiful,but even for twelve year olds it could still be earnt but it wasn't easy.Once a month I would trudge round the Rowner Naval Estate roads,be it light or dark,rain or shine, two hundred and fifty Wavy Line grocery leaflets needed feeding into hungry letterboxes.The reward, two and sixpence,or half a crown,not a vast sum to last the month,to provide bars of chocolate and a variety of comics.Although only a few pence each,the weekly issues of the "Beano Eagle,Topper and Dandy", to read about Roy of the Rovers,Korky the Kat,Gnasher,Minnie the Minx and Dan Dare,did not come cheaply.

 Thus it was that at various times of the year opportunities arose to build up larger sums,to supplement the monthly stipend,but rest assured it was long hours ,back breaking work and proved extremely tiring.At twelve years old it seemed very tempting,some would give up after a couple of days,but those that lasted the course reaped worthwhile dividends.The summer holidays presented the first of these opportunities,but to get to the work was in its own way quite an effort.Soon after first light,a hot day in prospect,I waited with my bicycle at the crossroads for my pals to arrive.One by one they arrived, and half a dozen in number,we headed up Rowner Road, thankful that we would get to the Newgate Lane turning, before the first Royal Navy Bedford low loaders, transporting complete aircraft to Fleetland's Repair Yard would start their journeys.Hawker Hunters,Sea Venom and various Westland Helicopters with folded wings and rotor blades were transported in this way from HMS Daedalus the nearby naval airfield. Cycling on through Stubbington,past the church and village green,round the bend past Crofton Manor farm and down the hill into Titchfield.It was here that we alighted to start work.Entering the fields we would be kitted out with plywood trays and small woven punnets and pointed into the direction of row upon row of strawberry plants.Each row was separated with straw,keeping the ripe fruit off the ground and stopping the field from getting too muddy if rain was to arrive,On hands and knees,only ripe fruit was picked and had to include the stalk attached,needless to say many were eaten by the pickers and our red lips soon gave the game away.Each full punnet was weighed,four,eight or sixteen ounces,the number of punnets were then counted and the appropriate payment made,before a weary ride home and bed only to return the next day to do it all over again.

Strawberry season over,the next opportunity was at Crofton Grange Farm,where in those days it was not so much "pick your own" but more of picking someone else's!

It was not quite so far to cycle and the work was less productive,pay wise, but pea picking was physically harder with constant bending over,whilst selecting full pods to fill a wooden tray, or cardboard trug, with a silver metal handle.It certainly paid havoc with the back,but sweet peas straight from the pea pods,carefully avoiding the maggots,made it bearable.

Both of these jobs prepared me for the real hard work which followed when summer was over, later in the year,and sorted out the men from the boys,although this was rather a misquote as much of the work was in fact performed by women.

Late August arrived and with it the back breaking chore of picking potatoes,the half hundred weight hessian sacks had to be filled with fifty five pound of potatoes.Potatoes, brought to the surface by the tractor using a type of harrow,were "'picked",dirt and all, often damaged they were all needed to fill the sacks.The tractor and trailer picked up the full sacks to be weighed,short weight ones didn't get paid so you soon learnt to slightly overfill them.A few days of this and you wished the end be soon,inevitably sooner or later it would rain,your back painfully aching,hands sore and either sunburned or soaked it was hard to think anything could be worse,in an effort to earn pocket money.There was,however a job to make even these agonies seem rather pleasant..

Come November at half term and weekends the new opportunity presented, even surpassed the discomfort of the potato picking.By now the autumnal weather would bring ,misty or foggy mornings with light drizzle and extreme cold heralding the sprout picking season.It was said that they should never be picked until "the frost had been on them" and this was often the case.The little green cabbages on their tall cane like stems were picked off one by one,they were cold,icy,wet and often slimy,you were cold wet and frozen to the marrow,wrapped in an

overcoat,wearing fingerless woollen gloves,balaclava and scarf,red cheeked and teeth chattering.
 Was it worth it...well we thought so,it was hard work,either too hot or too cold,and in the autumn the possibility of falling off your trusty,or rusty bicycle on the icy lanes was an added bonus.

++

 A vagrant,homeless,down and out,man of the road whatever you wished,all sad circumstances but in my childhood he was simply a tramp.We kids were fascinated by the untidy individual with his long white nicotine stained beard,weather beaten face and slow ungainly gait as he wandered the leafy streets.When you went out to play there was no fear of him but more a sense of awe and fascination.In his worn out shoes,brown felt hat and khaki brown ex-army overcoat tied with string,a flannel shirt under it for warmth he could be seen regularly in Gosport.Walpole Park,Stokes Bay,Stanley Park all provided shelter for him at various times.He would always chat if you gave him the chance,he was kind polite and happy to impart his knowledge to the children,his knowledge of the natural world truly amazing.We weren't afraid of him and we gave a lonely old man a reason to live,even if at time we teased him.He would readily impart his knowledge if you gave him time,and sit smiling as the children listened to his worldly tales,or played happily.He never begged but would gratefully accept worn out clothes and offers of food made by sympathetic people,he would readily offer work in return and when he did he took pride in his labours.
 Who was he,I know not,I have no idea of his name.I never saw him drunk and I never heard him complain.For many years I remember him walking in Gosport and Lee on Solent,keeping his own company seemingly happy in his own solitude.He slept on benches without fear and safe in the knowledge of little chance of being harmed.What became of him I do not know, but remember him as a kindly but slightly eccentric man who always gave me a kind word,not persecuted but a

welcome individual who had chosen an individual lifestyle.What a different attitude there was to the less fortunate,although he accepted sustenance,he never asked or expected it.He had made his lot and happily accepted it.I remember fondly that ancient character,he was a fixture of my childhood but sadly anonymous.

++

By the time the 1950's arrived and the weariness of battle had begun to recede, the menfolk had time on their hands and grasped the opportunity with open arms.Hobbies and pastimes became important once more and many of these had the added bonus of a little bit of spare cash from an enjoyable pastime.

Front gardens with immaculately manicured lawns suddenly appeared,patriotic flower beds in red,white and blue,red salvias,white alyssum and blue lobelia were the order of the day.The addition of these flowers and the fashionable purple aubrieta which graced the new popular rockeries competed with scented roses in a multitude of colours.The allotments were still an important vegetable source but along with greenhouses there was ample space to grow dahlias,chrysanthemum,sweet peas and carnations which were readily saleable to hungry florists.Dad had built up a ready trade in chrysanthemums and had managed to make a little garden which sported many plants and exciting areas in which to play.

Sport was as popular as ever,football,cricket,tennis,athletics and for the higher classes,hockey and rugby,or even lacrosse and other popular working class hobbies,pigeon racing,cage bird and rabbit showing were gaining pace,Their were pigeon lofts,Mr Shepherd had one in Leesland Road,and there was at least one in Norman Road,and aviaries popped up in various home made garden buildings,Budgies became extremely popular,but Dad bred canaries with their melodic songs and exotic names, Borders,Gloucesters,Yorkshires and Red Factors.Needless to say the birds were fascinating but the garden had untold riches and it was there that adventures were played out.The practice sessions with the blanket covered wooden clothes horse, under which we hid with a home made jam tart and glass of water in front of the fireplace were replaced with the real thing.This took the form of a dense rhododendron bush which you were able to enter and hide in its centre without being visible.The wished for "den" was here and I would take a picnic and toys into the centre, and hide away,giggling and laughing silently as the adults muttered "where's that boy now" as if they didn't know.

From the garden as I became older the dens stretched into parks and the countryside,where we could hide unseen, much to the annoyance of unsuspecting passers-by as we made mischief,at their expense.

+++

It was Monday morning,it was April and it was 1958.Up bright and early,black polished shoes neatly laced,long dark green socks held up with elastic garters complete with green flashes which showed when the socks were neatly turned over.Short grey trousers held up with a leather belt and metal clasp, topped with a green long sleeved pullover,plain to start with, but later adorned with various round or triangular cloth badges to show the disciples you were proficient in.Around my neck was tied a "neckerchief" in the pack colour held tightly in place with a leather woggle and crowning it was a green peaked cap with yellow tubing decoration.Not today the"dibbing" and "dobbing" of Tuesday night "parade",at the Nicholson Hall opposite The White Hart pub and the no 7 bus stop home.The evenings of learning knots or woodcraft,of collecting coins,stamps,cheese labels,matchboxes,even cigarette packets,of learning signs and solving problems was not for today,today was the start of "bob a job" week.Card and pencil in hand we would fearlessly knock on brass door knockers imploring the occupant "bob a job please"as we stood to attention ,giving the scout salute and then waited with anticipation.Simple tasks of polishing shoes,cleaning windows,sweeping the yard or pavement,even running errands,all were accepted and when satisfactorily completed were duly rewarded by the agreed compensation,sometimes as much as "half a crown".

The week ended and at next cub's parade we would vie to see who had collected the most money and chatter amongst ourselves about the more unusual tasks we had been asked to carry out.Coffers full we would get our reward at summer camp,a week in the wild,a field full of cows,inviting woodland and the inevitable babbling stream.Tents erected,groundsheets in place and allsettled in there was still plenty to do.Job allocation saw some with latrine spades digging the ditches for daily usage,suitably disguised with a canvas screen.Others dug an area out of the field for the campfire which was a necessity if we were to eat,even more collected firewood,fetched water,peeled potatoes and swung ropes over strong tree boughs,often projecting over the stream,to provide swings.Washing took place in the swift flowing stream,we were used to cold water, and after a meal and drink prepared in billy cans over the now roaring fire,we sat around the campfire for a"Gin Gan goolie goolie watcha".before retiring to bed.

The giggling and mischief continued till the early hours,ventures outside of the tents,raiding the other patrol tents,all carefully avoiding too close a contact with adult scouters.Up with the lark,breakfast of cereal,bacon and eggs,cooked over the fire,washing up duties,washing ourselves and then parade and the raising of the flag and sworn allegiance to the queen.

The day was spent learning about nature,carving wood,we all had our own sheath knives,visiting places of historical interest and visits to the village stores to send a postcard home,or maybe purchase a packet of bubblegum.

Great days to grow up,learn and grow older.

++

 School holidays were full of exciting times and children,like myself,spent nearly all their time out of doors be it summer or winter,rain or shine..So many hazardous obstacles to overcome and not a health and safety person in sight,we were meant to use our common sense and most of the time we did a remarkably good job of it.Traffic,generally at a sedate speed and people who walked at a brisk pace were not a major problem to us as we often went out of view from our adult guardians without any fears or worries,You walked facing oncoming traffic if there was no pavement,you looked left and right when crossing the road, with a giant squirrel,Tufty as a companion or later on a Giant Green Man.You avoided the odd car,crossed busy roads at zebra crossings marked with belisha beacons, jumped off moving buses,crashed your homemade soap boxes into the road and climbed walls,careful to pick the ones not topped with broken glass.You fell over and cried,picked yourself up, rubbed off the dirty grit,wiped it clean with spittle,visited accident and emergency if you were fifty percent dead,prepared for most eventualities by our common sense. Brambles were a major problem,they had thorns,nettles sting you but there was always a dock leaf nearby.Sharp needle like thorns were braved to pick wild rose hips,when dry their contents made great itching powder,
 We got thirsty,we drank crystal clear stream water,we got hungry we picked wild blackberries,hazel nuts,even sloes.In the hedgerows, we pulled up horseradish root for the roast beef and in the park on a dewy morning we would gather mushrooms for breakfast.The lack of supervision was made up by the knowledge our elders imparted....if only I had listened I would still be with you all now...c'est la vie!

++

I stood on the doorstep and watched gloomily as the small motor bike with its uniformed rider pulled up across the road,the neighbours curtains twitched as they tried to see.Alighting from his bike and pulling his uniform tidy the rider knocked at the door of a house opposite and removed a small envelope from his satchel.His appearance normally meant only bad news and as he reverently handed the missive to the occupant,who immediately opened it, you saw the tears welling in their eyes as they mumbled "thank you."The almost embarrassed telegraph boy,as that was what he was, politely moved away and remounted his transport,returning to the telegraph office for a hopefully happier telegram to deliver the next time.

The door closed,silence prevailed,onlookers returned indoors,curtains stopped twitching indoors speculation as to what had happened was rife.Respectfully everyone declined to venture to the recipient neighbour until an adequate amount of time had passed and it was felt to be polite.No phone call,very few phones,everything caring and very personal.I continued playing on the pavement,the mood rather sombre having sensed all was not as it should be,a foreboding sense to not be noisy.As the day progressed a flow of neighbours beat a path to the relevant house,all of them reappearing with solemn faces,stopping to quietly speak to each other,whispering in a manner not to alarm or frighten the children who played in the street.
Days later we may have had an inkling of the situation,the signs of a passing instantly recognisable,but in the main children were not told of grown up things,it was not for them.

++

Those of us that managed to survive the trials and tribulations of the constant threat of poisoning by the food we ate graduated to take part in level two.This one however was even more dangerous,in fact so dangerous that was probably why health and safety was conceived.I can vividly recall the urge of tasting various soft drinks with same label but of vastly different appearances.

 Packets and bags were the order of the day,the packets wouldn't have been a problem if the contents hadn't migrated to other containers."Go and get a biscuit" she said,wonderful idea thought I.During and after world war two the Ministry of Food had supplied full cream milk powder in silver[later white] tins with printed blue labelling.Each tin contained the equivalent of seven pints and had a striking resemblance to cream coloured dessicated coconut,with a distinctive odour.Going for the biscuits I opened the cupboard door and was confronted by what must have been every dried milk tin that we had ever purchased,best of all,they all said dried milk and nothing else,labels had never crossed Nana's mind.One by one the lids were prised off,rice,dried peas,semolina,dried fruit,macaroni,cream crackers,and at last custard creams and bourbon biscuits.The other tins could have contained I know not what but didn't need to be opened.Having had the biscuit I then discovered that this wasn't the total of these tins in existence.Throughout the cupboards and drawers tins were a dominant feature,storage containers were expensive and you made do with what was available.There was a button tin,a wool tin,a cotton tin,a pin tin,a tin for hooks and eyes,a tin for drawing pins,the variety was endless as were the tins.There were Colmans mustard tins,Oxo tins,St Bruno,Ogdens and Gold Leaf tobacco tins,Kiwi,Cherry Blossom and Wrens boot polish tins and they all contained different products to what they should have had.

 This array, however, was only surpassed by the contents of the garden shed.Order of the day was"make do and mend",but to do this, the items to effect the mend had to be stored.The shed was where the second division of dried milk tins suddenly appeared ready to create another smoke screen..There were tins with screws,washers,nails,wire,cup hooks,various tape,putty, and bits and bobs but none were labelled.Hours could be spent looking for"I know it's here somewhere" in fact so long it was enough to develop a thirst.Temptation to have a sip from one or two of the unlabelled bottle's contents,linseed,paraffin,turpentine,petrol.bleach,and even battery acid was without doubt contemplated,but never in fact succumbed to.

How I haven't ended up permanently damaged I know not,but we did tend to know what items were and what they were to be used for.Those re-used insignificant tins were a significant part of 1950's life,without them the make do and mend philosophy would have never survived.

++

The small uncut tin loaf was slightly stale and would need toasting before I ate it.Browned over the open coal fire,whilst still warm,it was spread with butter that had started to go"oily" and a deeper yellow,a certain sign of rancidity creeping in.The bottle of yesterday's milk,although kept in a bucket of water,had begun to thicken and when used in tea, little fat globules rose to the top of the cup.Never mind however, when used in my porridge it didn't taste at all once disguised with a couple of spoons of sugar.

Breakfast eaten, the last of the stale bread ,added to by other similar morsels from the enamel bread bin was left to soak in water,before wringing it out,adding spice and dried mixed fruit and using it to make bread pudding.Covered with a clean white cloth it would wait for its turn in the old gas oven Nan would go shopping and if it was holidays I would go out with a packed lunch neatly wrapped in greaseproof paper.

The little pack of sandwiches,normally cheese and tomato,were by the time they were to be eaten the consistency of wet cardboard.The tomato had "softened the bread to a liquid consistency,but in fairness made the"mousetrap"cheddar cheese,which had had the mould scraped off that morning,more palatable.This was often accompanied by a slice of stale madeira cake or "crusty" victoria sponge,sometimes a rock bun straight from the quarry face.

 On arrival at the butchers shop the unrefrigerated meat was starting to turn dark in colour as the blood oxidised and the grey mince and sausages made from yesterday's unsold meat had a slightly old odour about it,never mind, cook it well and it was safe enough.Along the road to the greengrocers to buy the misshapen vegetables,wholesome enough, but difficult to peel,and the turnips,swedes and potatoes had arrived with half the field attached.Peas came complete with maggots,cauliflower and cabbages with caterpillar passengers and bruised fruit looking as though it had been in a boxing match.Lemons with a green dusty mildew powder,bananas with black skins and apples

and pears with brown patches which had to be cut out and even then they sometimes had invaders inside.Even if you picked blackberries fresh from the hedgerows,or mushrooms,wild from a field when you washed them a maggot could be found desperately trying to swim in the remaining water.Even hazelnuts off the tree had neat holes in the shells betraying an unwanted addition to their contents.

 Back at the corner shop Nana would, if having enough spare money,select a fresh cream cake from a long wooden tray on the top of the warm shop counter.The delicious cream "was slightly on the turn" but who cares it was a special treat,slightly tainted"but it won't kill you" was the message.

 Teatime came, a piece of the now cooked,still warm,bread pudding,jam on buttered bread,but only after the mould had been scraped off both the bread,as well as the top of the jam jar, which when opened was found to have mould under the greaseproof paper top.The now not so fresh cream cake,the cream now a deep yellow and with a slight"twang",completed the tea.A broken biscuit before bed ensured we didn't go to sleep hungry.

I miraculously survived the fact that nobody had told anyone when an item should be sold by,when it should be used by whether it was off and even if it should have been thrown away.
 Common sense must have been the magic ingredient once again,if it smelt alright it probably was.

++

 The irritation was incessant,the passage of the little terrace led over a linoleum floor to steep,dark stairs,The weary ascent of the narrow stairs covered with a carpet runner held in place with polished brass stair rods,needed constant assistance from Nana.
 The fever and the itching rash had come on surprisingly quickly and even before the doctor arrived,measles had been the suspect.On arrival the eminent practitioner was ushered up to the double bedroom at the front of the house and removed his heavy outdoor coat.On the marble washstand stood a ewer of hot water,a bowl,soap and a crisp clean white towel ready prepared for the doctors use.Opening his bag he produced a rubber tubed stethoscope with chrome earpieces and a sound piece he placed on my back and then chest.The end which had been breathed on to warm it up,albeit to no avail was placed on my chest and the doctor listened intently as I was asked to take deep breaths and he tapped my back.A glass,mercury filled thermometer was then produced,shaken, and placed under the tongue after which came an inspection of the red rash which was increasing by the minute.
 "Measles,keep him in bed,curtains drawn,and not let him get too hot or scratch,use calamine lotion to relieve the itching and I'll be back next week".declared the physician.
 At this point he washed and dried his hands,donned his coat and was escorted to the door,I could then hear Nana climbing back upstairs and entering the bedroom,She put a bolster under the pillows to raise my head,rolled back the eiderdown leaving just the thin white sheets to cover my fever racked body.A cold flannel was placed on my forehead

and when I eventually dozed off to sleep I still found myself drifting in and out of a state of awareness.Constant nursing,supplying me with water and "Lucozade" to drink and continually tempting my appetite with chicken broth,soft boiled eggs with "soldiers" gradually renewed my strength,the itching had stopped and after a few weeks I was once again allowed to rejoin the real world.To leave that room,see light through net curtains,no longer view the watercolour prints on the bedroom wall of Faith,Hope and Charity,leaving the scent of eau-de-cologne and smelling salts behind was wonderful.No more the odd sniff of mothballs from the blanket box,or the sight of the white pressed linen runners topping the dressing table,on which stood a dressing table set in flowery transfer printed china.
I had survived and could live again!

++
 I had saved my pennies for weeks,the odd loose change usually half-pennies, and the deposits gained from returnable "pop" bottles foraged from wherever,The arrival of the gas meter man was a particular favourite, as you might get a "bob" from the money given back when the meter was emptied,so by the time I started the holidays I thought I was a rich man.My piggy bank was opened and the little piles of pennies were ready to be counted,the next time it would be opened would be at Christmas when it was time to purchase small presents.

 Having totalled up the coins,the question was how to spend them,save them to spend on a days outing,indulge in sweets or purchase a special item I had been eyeing up in the toy shop in North Street or Woolworths.It was the latter which I had decided on
this particular summer and a trip to Woolworths was definitely necessary.
 Amongst the multitude of plastic Airfix kits there was one that I had been watching longingly and now my chance had arrived.Most of the

model kits were in polythene bags but the one I wanted was in a large box,what made it most exciting it had an electric motor,it actually moved or in this case "voyaged"under its own power.

Running through the wooden floored shop chivvying Nana to keep up with me I came to the toy counter and it was still there.Nana helped me to select the expensive kit and I handed it to the assistant."Ten shillings and sixpence please", she said and I handed over my handful of change.The purchase was placed in a large paper bag,transaction complete,overcome with excited anticipation I couldn't get home quickly enough.

Once there,there was no time to waste,emptying the contents of the box straight onto the table,the construction of the motorised Landing Craft ,as that was what it was,could begin..A short enforced break for tea,then back to the task in hand before bedtime.The following morning I was"up with the lark"any delay was too long in my all consuming

passion to finish the construction,I wanted to use it.All completed,battery added and motor tested we were all ready to visit the test venue,Gosport Boating Lake was to be the place to give it its first trials.Clutching the little boat proudly in my hands and telling anyone and everyone about my prized possession we arrived at our destination.The water was a little choppy,even so I couldn't get the model in the water quickly enough.Placing it gingerly,a little nervous,I flicked the switch,pointed it across the lake and away it chugged,to my horror it seemed to be getting lower in the water and as it approached halfway across the lake I watched in dismay as it filled with water and vanished from view....for all I know it may still be there ...and when I think of it now the disappointment is still tangible,if slightly amusing.

++

Summer evenings saw a steady stream of people to the local public houses,when they would have "off sales",entered by an obscured door into a little passageway which held a wooden counter flap,nothing on the counter,but we could provide a jug from home and have it filled with draught beer.The advertisement on the glass door said "jug and bottle"with Brickwoods stout,porter.ale and beer advertised on the frosted glass windows,the ale bought as light.bitter,or brown dispensed from wooden casks lovingly made by the breweries cooper.To accompany the beverages a packet of Smiths potato crisps with blue wax paper twists of salt enclosed.The variety was limitless,salted or nothing,the only other alternative salted peanuts.As the old hand pumps became obsolete gas was needed to pump the manufactured beers,and flavoured crisps were developed with artificial chemically produced tastes. Hurriedly carried home, the men folk would consume the beer,pipes and cigarettes accompanying whilst the women imbibed in a tipple of homemade wine,parsnip,potato,or beetroot all made from vegetables grown on the allotment,or sometimes blackberry,damson or sloe gathered from the summer hedgerows.Us kids would sometimes have granny's lemonade or ginger beer,Bread and cheddar cheese made up the supper and the whole family would sit around the tiny bakelite radio,powered with it's clear glass batteries.I was more interested in watching the bubbles rising from the lead plates as the acid reaction produced the electric power. Simple programmes "Sing something Simple" with the Cliff Adams Singers,Charlie Chester,Wilfred Pickles and Mabel,Terry Thomas,Professor Jimmy Edwards,Dick Barton special agent,Round the Horn,The Navy Lark to name just a few. Simple food and drink,simple programmes and certainly simpler people.Not people with simple intellect but people with simple tastes and simple needs,a simpler life but simply happier for it.

++

 Opposite Gosport War Memorial Hospital,an imposing pebble dashed building,with a red tile roof and an elegant pillared entrance above which was an equally elegant clock, stood a small parade of shops.In this parade,on the corner of The Avenue,were a Co-op and a chemist and diagonally opposite on the corner of Ann's Hill Road and Privet Road stood the Wiltshire Lamb public house,a rather salubrious "spit and sawdust affair".A little further down on the same side stood the more select Harvest Home hostelry where a slightly more respectable clientele would imbibe their ale.The fire station,flanked with a high concrete water tower stood almost opposite and if you then turned back towards the hospital you came to the rather affluent avenue.On the corner of The Avenue was a small area of rough pasture which would occasionally have a pony or two tethered on it.The Avenue,itself, boasted mansion like, turn of the 20th century houses on the left hand side fronted with sweeping gravel drives and extensive residential accommodation.

 Towards the end of the tree lined avenue,before you reached the old Alverstoke cemetery which held graves stretching back to the eighteenth century, there was one of the largest of these houses,owned by Mr John Hunt,a tall gentleman with a handlebar moustache and black rimmed glasses.He drove an Armstrong Siddeley Sapphire and with his brother Pat,a giant of a man with blonde hair and a trademark sheepskin coat,who fashionably drove a large gold coloured Jaguar Mark 10 had built up a building company of some repute.Ministry of Defence work was plentiful and paid well and such contracts were actively sought after.Sultan,Daedalus,Collingwood,Frater,Bedenham,Fleetlands,Priddy' Hard and Clarence Barracks all displayed work they had done.The diving tower at Haslar was their work as too was a lot of work at ASWE on the top of Portsdown Hill.The later was possibly however better remembered by me for the many wild orchid varieties I was introduced to growing in its secure fences.Frog,Bee,Spider,Early Purple Pyramid and Spotted,all grew on the chalk land turf and I often wonder if they are still there..

Civvy street projects included the famous "Rising Sun" public house at Clanfield which was built in a day and featured on Reuters News and the innovative tower block flats at Wingfield Street in Portsmouth.
The common factor,beside the builders,on all these projects was the site agent,Gerry,my dad.

++

What a pickle!!
Skipping along the pavement,minus rope,I entered Mr Hornes' emporium.not dissimilar to others dotted on most street corners in most of Gosport,crammed with all the items a modern 1950;s housewife would need.Clutching two old pence in one hand and a white china jug in the other I reached up to the top of the counter and the friendly smiling,moustached face of the proprietor leant down to my level and smiled."can I have a pint of vinegar please" I asked holding up the copper pennies and jug.Taking both from me,he walked to a wooden barrel,turned the tap,and ran a pint of the brown pungent liquid into the waiting receptacle.I gingerly gripped the jug in both hands,one holding the handle and the other cradling the short snub spout ,"You go careful and don't spill it" said the friendly man as he assisted me out of the brown glass paned door and watched me slowly and deliberately make my way seven doors up.Standing at the doorstep I called out "Nana" and waited till the said grey haired lady came and rescued the jug with its un-spilt contents.Having handed over the jug I sat on the doorstep waiting for the smell of pickle to waft from the scullery as chutney boiled in the preserving pan.

++

I met John Clare for the first time in the later 1950's and he soon became a good friend since those early years,,in fact ever since my childhood in those later years of that decade.He would always listen quietly to the things I had been seeing and doing,speechless as I told him of the sounds,smells and beauty that I had experienced walking through the lanes and fields,something he,himself,had experienced Painted Ladies,Large and Small Coppers,Red Admirals and Peacocks flew invitingly in fragrant meadows,their bejewelled wings beating in timeless motion,Meadow Sweet,Rue,Wild Thyme and Mint pervaded the air as it was crushed underfoot and its aromatic odours floated on the air.

In hedgerows the distinct music of Nightingales,Blackcaps and Whitethroats punctuated the air as dusk approached by,accompanied by the harsher sounds of Cuckoos and Nightjars, eclipsed as the darkness finally fell, by the shriek of the Barn Owl's call.

In the giant Oak myriads of insects,beetles and caterpillars had

made their homes ensuring the futures of the many dependents that relied on them to survive.

With the red sky heralding the night, turning pink,then orange the fluffy cumulus clouds silently drifted across the darkening sky.We watched in awe as planets and constellations lit up the dark heavens as tiny pinpoints of light.

To myself and John these treasures were everyday treasures to be loved,cherished and protected so future generations could enjoy the wonderful sights.Our knowledge was the key,a key which now seems to be broken in the lock,a key which seemed to have been lost over the last sixty years.

The reason why John was speechless?.......Well John Clare was the peasant poet,one of the best ever poets, who had died not in the 1950's, but the 1860's.....one hundred years and so very little had changed...sixty years later and I don't need to comment!

++

As I took a step over the brass covered sill and onto the bleached white step at the front door the sun shone straight down the street as it always did.Dreamily,with nothing particularly in mind I ambled down the road and then back again.My attention was drawn to tiny movements in between the cracks in the pavement little ants were coming up for air surrounded by little piles of freshly excavated sand,occasionally transporting a white egg or pulling a small piece of debris back into their nest.Scurrying backwards and forwards they worked tirelessly moving around the stone slabs of the pavement with ease.Along the pavement edges hand hewn granite stones divided the path from the metalled road which in places had small pools of melting black tar

Looking along the length of the road there were no cars to be seen and it was eerily silent,maybe the odd silent passage of a bicycle,otherwise just the sound of wing beats from the pigeons
wheeling around having been released from a loft in an adjacent road.Suddenly there was a louder distant sound.a hum as a bus entered the road from the distant t-junction,followed by a noisier clank of a tipper lorry from Treloar's yard making its way to some demolition site nearby.

One or two people began to emerge as I sat on the doorstep watching the ants and hoping one of the boys from no 74 would come out to play.I ventured back indoors and re-emerged with some Dinky cars and set about imaginatively playing out various scenarios whilst I patiently waited.A striped caterpillar appeared on the path and I watched as the ants explored the new invader but too busy to really bother they carried on their daily tasks and left the future butterfly to slowly crawl away looking for its next plant meal.This in such a sterile area was no easy task as weeds as well as human litter played no part in the pavements or gutters which were daily swept by the road sweeper.No place either for white and yellow lines to deface the roads and only basic street signs appeared at road junctions.No need for no waiting signs and the smaller road junctions had no signs at all,no stop signs,no give way signs,in fact the road names were the most prominent labels as they jostled with the enamel advertising signs for Lyons Cakes,Brooke Bond Dividend Tea or Oxo which adorned the walls of the corner shop.My musings were interrupted by the arriving sound of a large red articulated Co-operative milk lorry,chains rattling and bottles clinking as it stopped outside no 90 and Mr Weaver,a tall man in brown overalls went in for his breakfast as he did every day."alright lad" he would say and politely I would reply "Yes thank you".A voice from inside the house said"who was that"."Mr Weaver" I replied."Well keep your eye out Mr.Shepherd will be here in a minute and I don't want to miss him" I never mastered the logic in that statement as a man with a horse pulling a cart laden down with green grocery was hardly likely to slide in unseen and unheard.

++
 The lady with the blue rinse and glasses from no 76 quietly appeared, Mrs Lawrence,bespectacled,always smiling,with cloth in hand began to vigorously clean the already gleaming windows.Soon she was joined by one of the Miss Reads,there were two sisters,from no 78,then Mrs King,a tall lady,tall enough to see over the garden wall into Nanas backyard, to tell me off for my ball hitting her window,was the resident at no 82 who began to scrub their doorsteps.Mrs King looked over and said"you waiting for the boys,they won't be long" as it was her grandsons who lived with their mum,Eileen,at no 74,that I was waiting for.Cleaning finished they stopped to have a natter and gossip,several had cigarettes dangling from the corner of their lips only removing them to pass the time of day with other local residents.Mrs Edwards,a short lady,always with a slight grin,and a trademark costume of curlers and red lipstick,cigarette in hand, married to the gasman, would exit no 88 and call in at no 84.She popped in every morning where her even shorter mother Mrs Pavey, a delightful,frail bespectacled grey haired lady resided.From no 86 would emerge my aunt Mrs Ada Elliott,from no

98 another aunt Mrs Amy Smith and from no 100 my uncle Mr Bert Fowler.The two ladies lived alone but Uncle Bert was married to my Auntie Ada who was sadly struck down with Parkinson's Disease and a more devoted husband you could not wish to meet.Sometime during every morning they would all make their way to Mr Horne's corner shop on the junction with Norman Road.Next door to the shop lived Mr Weaver's brother and this shop was where we all went for our"convenience items"safely in the capable hands of Mr and Mrs Horne,a lovely happy couple.Mr Horne a dapper,round faced,cheerful man,slightly balding with grey hair and black rimmed glasses,always wearing a beige linen jacket and bow tie.Mrs Horne was a short,slightly plump lady as was her husband and he was only slightly taller than her,she had grey hair in a swept back style,glasses and always dressed in a flower patterned full length pinafore.

 The opposite side of the road had several notable residents,Mr and Mrs Lucas lived in a big detached house almost opposite the shop,Mrs Yates,the churchwarden,next door,Mr & Mrs Clogg and Norma Rooke a little further up past Mrs Sands and Mrs Shepherd who owned the flower shops.Norma was related to the Miss Reads but I don't know in what capacity.I have no recollection of Mrs Clogg but her husband sticks clearly in my memory.He owned the hardware shop in Whitworth Road and was a kind,gentle man with a twinkle in his eye.He walked with a stoop and shuffling gait using a walking stick due to the built up boot on one foot,he was always dressed in black and had a long white beard,steadily puffing on a trusty briar which yellowed his facial hair.The last two people I recall, both tended the florist shops previously mentioned incorporated in the front room of Mrs Sands house,next door Mrs Shepherd's shop a lean-to conservatory built on the right hand side of her house,with shelves to hold the vases of flowers.Often when you went to purchase there was no assistant but all the flowers were priced and there was an honesty box on the counter.Additionally Mrs Shepherd would stock a small selection of fruit for people to take with a bunch of flowers if you were visiting the hospital to see a patient Mrs Sands Shop was entered down a short passageway and she was a true character,a very down to earth person she had sharp but warm features,wore glasses,spoke with a deep gravelly voice,like her teeth her hair was stained yellow hair from the nicotine produced by her chain smoking habit.She was always most helpful and would pop out the back to the greenhouse where they grew their own flowers to get something special for that notable occasion if it wasn't immediately visible.

++

It was a cold misty February morning,I arose with no intention of doing much at all.Far from my thoughts was to go on an unplanned journey, and least of all one with no definitive destination.I was alone,not lonely,with no prospect of company as the family were away and I was at home to look after the harlequin Great Dane lying beside me.In that sense I wasn't on my own but conversation was limited as he hadn't mastered the ability to speak and my "woofs" seemed to not be effective,so I turned to see what I could do.
  As I started out I began to think of what I could remember from years before,my memories,some good and some best filed away.It occurred to me that the insidious ravages of time in the forms of memory loss,dementia and Alzheimer's disease would have an affect on some individuals unluckier than myself.Isolation takes many guises and loneliness may very well be no fault of the individual,more likely the fault of their circumstances.
  Tentatively I took the first steps outside and conveyed my memories to people I encountered, passing strangers,who knew nothing of me,and I,nothing of them.Gradually, they would,after the initial awkwardness start to converse and I became conscious that my personal memories were not dissimilar to their own.As I travelled to other far flung places it became apparent that even people from

different towns and villages also had similar memories,memories from the same times,of the same things, but in very different places.

Many seemed to be digging into their own personal memory bank,jogged into life by my own simple recollections and most significantly sharing them with others.Casual acquaintances talked about these events to older relatives and smiling recognition invaded their,otherwise,empty faces,simply they remembered.As I trod the pathways,pouring out more and more frivolous information,the people on my journey joined in and we visited,fields,shops,rooms and streets,we experienced animals,birds,insects,plants and trees which we had mislaid in our minds.To some,hopefully, being lonely became less despondent as the realism struck home that there were other people in their memories who would like to share with them the most important thing they possessed from the past.One day,inevitably,the journey will stop,nobody will reach the end,some will fall by the wayside,unable to continue for all manner of reasons.I am certainly not finished with my memories and thoughts but like this book,written precisely for these reasons I have outlined,the memory journey doesn't end,it just means we have to pass the baton to the next person.

I discovered this because somebody who had been a friend in the past prompted my own memories and provided the platform to share them with others. I was curious but thought that I would relate some simple memories to see if I was able to jog the memories of the many lonely people, and help them recall their own experiences.

Dave Rowland was one of my group of friends when he arrived in Gosport from Reading in the early sixties.Unfortunately as I moved from Gosport we lost touch and he had never entered my mind until the last few months.

For a while I had been searching in my memory to find an opportunity to talk about a pastime or two which took up a large amount of my time in the early 1960's,growing up.It must have started in 1961 when I was leaving primary school to carry on my education at grammar school and most of my school pals were moving on to Brune Park Secondary

School.During weekends,evenings and large periods of the school holidays we would reconvene our friendships at Privet Park where we would plot our next adventures and play football or cricket.I wish the circumstances were happier but I feel that Dave,no longer with us,would chuckle at the thought that he was remembered from all that time ago.

My first recollections were of a slight,wiry,wide-eyed lad who was of a slightly nervous disposition,always laughing to cover up his nerves.He was not in any way a sportsman so his visits to our football games were rather as a spectator than a participant.If,on occasions we were short of players he would be press ganged into participating sometimes with unexpected consequences,This could be a surprise goal or a shriek as he tried to escape the ball as it was passed to him and several burly challengers bore down.

More often he would be found discussing music or groups and I remember his interest in it then,along with that of trains,as many

of us were "trainspotters".The group of us,Dave included,would visit Fareham Station,travel to Eastleigh to the engine works or railway sheds,even travel to Reading or Salisbury to watch the Castles,Halls and Manors thunder down the GWR mainlines.As steam locomotives became obsolete we would visit Cashmore's scrapyard on Barry Island.We would clutch notebook and biro-pen taking down numbers to add to the Ian Allan shed books or combined volumes which listed all the locomotives,Dave would always spot what we all missed and would studiously examine the locos whereas the rest of us were just content with taking numbers

Packed lunches were shared by us all,they were great times,lasting memories and I hope Dave that over the years you have also been able to look back with fond and cherished thoughts.Our paths were very different but without them having crossed again none of my writings would exist.R.I.P....Sixty years ago and I can still remember you!

++

Anticipation had been rising everyday since last Thursday's weekly shopping trip.The regular day for shopping was as normal a journey made by number seven bus from the bus stop opposite the Co-operative grocers, on the corner of Kingston Road, situated along from Leesland School outside the Central School next door.The account had been paid,next week's grocery order placed,so onto the green Provincial bus we clambered, on our way to the High Street,via Stoke Road and Walpole Road before alighting outside the Gosport public library.As we passed Walpole Park,there it was,regularly as clockwork it would appear and I would peer longingly out of the bus window,over the old dry moat,past the Ritz cinema and then it disappeared from view again as we alighted at our stop.We hurried along to the shops but we didn't mind, as on the return journey we would have the chance of getting another glimpse of the exciting prospect of what we might visit over one of the next few days.Rejoining the bus at the Ferry Gardens,having paid a necessary trip to the pebble-dashed block of public toilets I was so excited I hardly had time to catch my breath.The rattling bus made its way up the High Street and past the library and there it was.....the fair was in town..hurrah hurrah! Wistfully gazing at the little village which had grown up in Walpole Park I began to pester"when can we go,when,when" to which the reply was"we'll see if your good".Forlornly I peered back as the fair faded from view and had that hopeless feeling that I would never get to visit it with its collection of rides and stalls,the cost far from my mind. The weekend had passed and although I pestered continuously it was always greeted with"we'll see",that was until Tuesday morning when Nana said"we'll go to the fair tonight if you are good today"The flood of joy,excitement,imagination and anticipation was immeasurable and the day was one of euphoria,Five o'clock didn't arrive soon enough,Dad picked us up from Leesland Road and the drive to Walpole Park took forever,we parked near the gasometers and I ran dragging the adults across the grass to the beckoning lights.We passed the caravans and fairground lorries,passing ferocious looking dogs which were chained to some of the showman's caravans.Passing through the perimeter ring of these ancient looking vehicles we entered the inner sanctum,the fair itself.Large coloured light bulbs,red,yellow,blue,green,red and white flashed endlessly to a thumping background of music from the rides and the shouts of"roll up,roll up" from the stall holders.

  Pink sticky candy floss,toffee apples with reddish brown sticky toffee.hot dogs with delicious smelling onions, the hot salted peanut machine dispensing it's wares into white paper bags,refreshments in abundance.

  Clutching a sample of one or more I headed towards the rides,sticky residue adorning my lips and chin.The Ghost Train was steered away from but their was a Hall of Mirrors,colourful horses galloping around the carousel,Swinging Boats,a Ferris Wheel and the Dodgem Cars.The latter manned by young workers,teddy boy haircuts, jumping from car to car,trying to impress the young ladies,avert crashes and collect the fares.All the time there was a background hum of generators powered by giant lorries,tinny music,constant laughter and chatter and the stallholders endless persuasiveness to part us from our hard earned money.As the evening hastened to an end gaggles of people clutching,chalk dogs,goldfish in glass bowls and those infamous flying ducks made their way home.Shooting ranges,fishing rubber ducks from a pool,throwing bent darts in a board or at playing cards,throwing rings over hooks...all the odds stacked against us winning,even the coconut shies.Needless to say tired,poorer people left the fair,but what enjoyment and happiness we all experienced in those efforts to win something and avoid the disappointment in returning empty handed.

++

Last night I pushed open the heavy glass door,stepped onto the footpath and ventured out into the bustle of the homeward bound army of people.That was the first difference between now and 1959,in fact you could be forgiven for thinking you were in a different world and that was almost true.Apart from the location being the same nearly everything had changed.The door,back then, would have been a wooden one and the sight of a seventy year old leaving work would also have been relatively unusual,in fact it was almost as long as most people lived.The fact that I was leaving an office based position answering phone calls for the ever elderly population to try and assist them in everyday life, with the never ending problems of mobility and dementia or alzheimer's, would in the 1950's have been unheard of.

  The walk to the car park led me to thinking just how much had changed and this train of thought continued as I made the short journey home.Getting into my car I thought back to that era of not so long ago.As I pressed the button to open the car door and then again to start the engine I lamented the fact that at least when I had an old fashioned key that I felt I was the one in control.The little box with a knurled nut you turned on to operate the tortoise speed windscreen wipers had long gone.

  As I pulled away, pondering on the fact that the faceless people I had left at work were treated by many,including their own families, as a nuisance and burden. I hankered back to when the elderly were treated with respect and reverence and they were the responsibility of loving families and not everybody else.

  With these thoughts in mind I started on my journey home,a journey of a distance from Brockhurst Road to Newgate Lane and I had two options.My first option was one which fifty years before would not have been there.A fast dual carriageway littered with traffic lights,roundabouts,yellow lines,white lines signposts,advertisements and various roadside debris from accidents,people's detritus littering the roadway or the corpse of some poor unfortunate creature which had had it's life abruptly ended.As the masses hurtled home in tin boxes they were oblivious to the creatures they unwittingly killed,be it animals,birds or the flying insects adhered to the front of their radiators when they reached their destinations.

 This thought lasted only fleetingly, so I opted for the more leisurely second option,a route which took me down country lanes and passed fields,more akin to my fifty year old memories.Alas as I made my way, this route too was almost unrecognisable.Ditches were no more managed nor were the hedgerows,many filled in or cut down.Five bar wooden gates to the field entrances had been supplanted by pieces of no longer used farm machinery.No more was a simple sign saying no trespassing or no entry suffice to stop individuals or groups usurping the farmland.The labourer who had attended the roadside verges with billhooks,scythes and sickles,his bicycle lent against a tree,canvas bag with his daily sustenance hanging from the handlebars was no more.What hedgerows were left had been flayed to death with a chain flail operated by a tractor,the driver had little or no knowledge of what flora or fauna was at arms length,in fact had probably never heard the words.

 Further along was the farmyard entrance bereft of the benches which would have had the milk churns stacked on them waiting to be picked up by the milk lorry,now refrigerated tankers performed the task if a dairy farm still existed.Missing too,on the the bench were new laid eggs,which you provided your own paper bag,yes paper,or bowl to carry them home in.It didn't matter if they were white or brown,large or small or even a little soiled,they were fresh.At times green top unpasteurised milk or cream would be present but no longer is this the case.Something else was missing,no animals,no cows chewing the cud or the cowpats that teemed with insect life after a few days in the field.Even the crops were different.Golden fields of sun dried wheat barley or quaking oats flecked with blood red field poppies had been replaced with soulless acres of sterile yellow rape flowers.Even green meadows,still needed for hay,were now devoid of life other than grass,all else destroyed by the overuse of "ides",fungicide,pesticide and insecticides.

By now I had arrived at my own little oasis in the countryside,in the past it would have been in Rowner Lane, but maybe reflecting I would have been better taking that modern dual carriageway,there would have been less time to rue the past's lost memories!

++

Clouds of choking dust and chaff billowed over the hedges.The people walking the footpath didn't matter and in fact the source of the pollution probably never even knew they were there.Another travesty of progress and realism that meant you were not really welcome but more of a blot on the landscape that believed it was owned by the perpetrator of the insidious dust Summer had arrived,swifts and swallows sailed across Leesland Road and when tired of feeding on the insects in the nearby cemetery they rested on the few new fangled telephone wires which stretched across the street.A lucky few houses played hosts to the little birds as they built their tiny cupped nests under the eaves of the terraced houses.In those days it was counted as lucky,nowadays they are more likely to be shooed away as "messy",or a nuisance.

We had packed our picnic in the trusty knapsack and having made our way to Lee-on-the-Solent we passed the main thoroughfare and headed to Hillhead and the twists and turns leading towards Titchfield Haven.The first part of the adventure was going down Monks Hill, freewheeling down the incline with it's Scots Pine and steep sandy banks on either side,and at the bottom glimpsing the sea through the line of wooden beach huts.

Heading along the road which edged the sea we would,if the tide was out and the sandy beach exposed,dismount, laying our bikes on the verge,and look for cockles.The tell tale signs of a hole accompanied by a jet of water saw us scrabbling feverishly before the cockle went too deep.At times razor shells reared up before digging themselves in the sand.Although close to Southampton Water and its traffic of ocean liners and oil tankers heading for the docks or Fawley Oil Refinery these small shellfish were still clean enough to be eaten.Having caught very few we decided to give them their freedom and try again on the return journey if the tide "was right".

 Back on the bicycles we headed to the whispering beds of swaying reeds where the River Meon ran under the road to meet the sea,then proceeded parallel to the river up a little narrow lane in the direction of the village of Titchfield.As we made our way we became aware of the sound of machinery coming from a high hedged field to our right.Approaching the field entrance we braked,stopped and feasted our eyes.Stood in the part harvested corn field were stooks of corn, gathered and stood to dry after being cut using a primitive Fordson or Ferguson tractor and harvester.A tractor and trailer circuited the next field and men were tossing the previous days sheaves,now dry,onto the trailer with pitchforks.It would then transport them to a long clanking red machine standing at the edge of the fields, powered by a standing traction engine and puffing,panting and clanking with a mind of it's own.Around these field edges stood flat capped,shirt sleeved individuals,some armed with shotguns,ready to dispose of foxes and vermin or to provide the bonus of meat for the pot from the escaping rabbits,hares,pheasants and partridges.Back at the red machine the dry corn was being threshed and the chaff separated from the ears of clean corn which in turn filled open hemp sacks.These sacks were placed in a horse drawn cart and then transported to the granary,stood on staddle stones at the nearby Abbey Farm or even to Botley flour mill for milling.The corn stalks meanwhile were thrown onto a hay cart and taken on to a storage area known as a rick field normally adjacent to the farm yard to be used for bedding for the farm animals.

 It was now fifty years later and the clouds of choking dust was also the result of the harvest in the same fields we had lain in many years before.No hedgerows around small neat fields but one vast shrubless area.No men with guns,no stooks,only two or three people encased in large air conditioned cabs of shiny flailing machinery. All in one the operation is now performed, clouds of invading dust, the farmhands ignorant of any wildlife, little as it now was, as it frantically tried to regain its freedom from the ever approaching mechanical monster.

The men in the air conditioned cabs ignorant of people and wildlife just hell-bent on finishing the job, ready to plant the next crop. No wonder the countryside is now becoming so sterile as the processes have been removed from nature's every day existence. Progress again seems to have relieved us of those joyous times when birds bees and butterflies played such a large part in all our lives.

++

It was hot, very, very hot and I really wanted to get home. I alighted from the maroon City of Portsmouth trolleybus in rather a sweaty dishevelled state. The cricket match had been a disaster and the ride from the Guildhall had been hot and sticky, to make things more deplorable, the hordes of dockyard workers on annoying bicycles were descending on the Gosport Ferry at the same time. When it was hot and sultry you dragged yourself along the causeway passed Portsmouth and Southsea railway station, the only things of interest, as you dodged the bicycles, being the odd steam engine in the station, or the mudlarks scrambling for the small change tossed into the pungent mud by the homegoing hordes when the tide was out. As the penny or halfpenny was retrieved by the mud encrusted larks they would hold it up smiling their thanks and whooping with delight. As we dragged our weary bodies nearer to the ticket office we thought little about these children and how important a part their few muddy pence played in keeping poverty from their families doors. To myself and others they were just comical entertainment to laugh at.

Reaching the ticket office, a little shed pitched in the middle of the ramp leading to the pontoon,I paid my half fare,and my paper ticket firmly clutched in my sweaty palm I proceeded to the bobbing pontoon.Interminably you seemed to be waiting,jostled and pushed by the dockers and their cycles.Arriving on the pontoon the boat was waiting,having disgorged its passengers it had brought from Gosport.It was on this occasion,a green and cream painted steam ferry,the "Venus",its boiler powered steam engine keeping it "on station"as I climbed up,the rope woven fenders protecting the paint as it bobbed around on the sea.Avoiding the now stacked bikes and at the same time standing as near to the bow as possible to ensure you would be one of the first off on the other side you waited for the crewman to cast off..Crammed on the deck the metal chains were closed around the side,health and safety would have had a fit,and black smoke belching from the funnel a crewman unhooked the heavy rope from the iron stanchion.We would reverse away and then set course,avoiding the paddle steamers sited on the railway station pier and steam between them and the two elderly Isle of Wight ferries which seemed to be permanently moored in open water just off the pier.Depending on water traffic you at times drifted towards the harbour entrance going close to the minesweepers moored in H M S Vernon or the entrance to the Camber Docks, in order to go astern of a mighty warship entering the harbour.Crossing the wash you would need to hold onto any available support as the turbulence would make standing up rather perilous,whole groups of passengers would lurch in any given direction and clutch each other to stand upright.On arriving at the Gosport side as soon as the chains fell apart I jumped off, running up the pontoon,sometimes catching sight of grey mullet lurking in the dappled sunlight under the floating piers,but most intent on not missing my bus.Running past the ticket office there would be a man selling newspapers from a little stand inscribed "Evening News".He was dressed in a dirty beige mac,greasy peaked cap and was unshaven,roll up cigarette hanging from his lips he shouted "read all the latest",always polite with a"thank you governor" as he received your money,Tucking the money into his coat pocket he quickly folded the next paper to replace the broadsheet paper, folded in half and half again which he had passed to the previous purchaser.who had proceeded to his or her bus where they would avidly sit and read.I headed for the number seven, normally a double decker,or the no six a single decker,the one to Leesland Road.

++

The green Provincial buses with gold copperplate script along the side lined up next to the public toilets,completely devoid of crew who were usually partaking of tea in The Dive,a greasy spoon cafe,opposite.The darker two tone green Hants and Dorset buses also inscribed in gold on the side[but squarer lettering] were in a separate parking area at the rear of the bus rank.If it was a hot day Hants and Dorset had their open deck buses in service,ideal to travel to Lee on the Solent,a really lovely journey along the seafront approaching Lee with a cooling seabreeze.The number six was the favourite as its route went up Leesland Road and I became such a familiar sight that the driver would drop me outside Nana's door about fifty yards from the recognised stop.Some evenings,when it came to six o'clock and I was rather slow getting to the bus stop, the driver would stop and toot the horn,waiting for me to emerge from no 80 so that I didn't miss the last bus to Rowner.The single decker would go up Southcroft Road,into Kingsland Road then Middlecroft Road and Cambridge Road before turning into Military Road.Proceeding to Brockhurst then down Rowner Road into St Nicholas Avenue,right into Mansfield Road and the driver would drop me off at the entrance gates which ran along the back of the shops in Rowner Lane.Through the gates and up the stairs to the flats above the shops where we lived at that time as Dad owned the grocers shop beneath.The fish and chip shops aroma was beguiling,the other shops less so as they consisted of an electrical shop,wine

shop,newsagents,bicycle shop,chemist and butchers[who also sold fruit and veg]
  By 1964 a lot of these experiences were no longer as trolley buses were no more,Nana had passed away and we had moved from the flat in Rowner Road to a bungalow nearby,but while it lasted it was a great adventure.

++

  Having watched the steam engines slowly travel down to Gosport Station,pulling the daily goods wagons,I longed to have the chance to have a ride on the footplate of one.As a family we had little reason to go anywhere on a train.short journeys were on foot,longer ones were by bus and if it was a day out or holiday Dad would use his car.
  This particular summer in the mid 1950's.however.I would have my dream come true,or almost,but under circumstances far from ideal and totally unexpected,in fact much of it sixty years on is still like living a dream.
  On this occasion we had travelled to Preston as we did every August but this time as we drove there in the blue and white Hillman Minx there was an extra air of excitement.We were only stopping overnight at Nan and Grandad's house as the following morning our journey was to continue.Up bright and early we said our farewells,climbed in the car,laden with luggage and headed on the road to Liverpool.The trip was fairly uneventful except for the part which took us through the Mersey Tunnel and coming out the other side we drove to what was similar to a large bus garage.The car was parked in this garage and we made our way to the docks and the ferry that was to take us to Dublin.Apart from remembering torrential rain and high winds making the sailing very unpleasant we arrived in Ireland memories of which were few.I remember lovely soda bread spread thickly with butter,alongside detestable white cabbage and bacon.Most vivid memories however were seeing the chickens in the kitchen,sometimes

joined by a pig or two and people who spoke in a language that to me was totally a foreign tongue.

After a dismal week we returned to Liverpool with weather still wet and miserable and made our way to collect our car from where it was parked.Packed back in we started out along the road enroute to Nan and Grandads in Preston.The heavy rain had now become a violent storm and through the heavy rain,the wipers struggling to clear the screen,there appeared a pick up van being filled with petrol from a can.As we approached there was a violent clap of thunder and Dad pulled out to overtake the stationary van,at that point a car appeared coming towards us and then it happened...Dad pulled back in and braked but nothing happened...I remember Dad flinging his arm across in front of me,shouting, and then nothing till I became aware of being in somebody's front garden. I must have been helped out of the crumpled vehicle and was taken into a house,and an ambulance arrived followed by a police car.After the chaos calmed down the ambulance drove off,bell ringing as it went,Dad was on his to Preston Infirmary,we were told he would be ok but I wasn't convinced.I remember the kind lady as she helped us to the police car to rejoin our luggage but little of the journey to Nan's in Preston where I was taken straight to bed.How long I was there I don't recall but eventually Dad arrived,his wounds patched,fortunately not too serious and we began to make plans to return to Gosport.

We arrived at Preston station.a high roofed edifice with elaborate cast ironwork and it was here my wish came true as there at the head of the train for Euston London was a monster of a steam engine "Duchess of Montrose"a Coronation class locomotive immaculate in gold lined maroon livery.Circumstances far from ideal and Dad's injuries still painful it would be several weeks later before we would make the return journey to hopefully recover the repaired Hillman.

++

Rich at last,I had been given a crisp brown ten shilling note and I was itching to spend it,Birthdays only came once a year and mine was close to Christmas.meaning very often my present was a "joint" one and birthdays were low key,but this time I was lucky!! I never had birthday parties although I do remember my older sister having them,my only jelly and blancmange was if I was invited to somebody else's...my birthday was just too close to Christmas!
  Thus it was that on the Saturday morning after my birthday I stood at the bus stop in Whitworth Road protected from the biting cold by a balaclava hat,scarf and gloves waiting for the no seven bus to take me to Gosport town centre.In my pocket was the ten shilling note and I was intent on spending it,The bus arrived and I climbed onto the rear platform before stepping up a fairly high step into the downstairs salon.Upstairs was out of the question as Nana's legs weren't good so we took the bench seat near the rear which ran down the side of the bus as you got in,A 'ding-ding" of the bell as the portly grey haired conductress in her bottle-green "trouser suit" and peaked cap pushed the button to signal to the driver "all was well" and off we moved.

'"Fares please" came the cry from the conductress and tendering the few pennies required,Nana would ask for "one and half" returns to the library please.The dial would be set,the handle cranked and a flimsy paper ticket printed in purple ink would disgorge itself.Torn off and given to the purchaser,Nana checked to ensure it was marked "R" for return.Away went the jolly conductress with a "Thank you...next please" whistling tunefully as she progressed down the bus,before returning to ride on the rear platform and engaging the adjacent passengers in conversation.Saturday morning the buses were always full and by the time we reached the White Hart Public House I would be standing, having respectfully given up my seat to an adult...the done thing in those days for a well-mannered child.The stopping and starting of the bus,coupled with slow progress due to the yellow pea-souper fog of the fifties winters,meant you were glad to see the library building appear from the gloom.As I alighted from the bus I remember well the fresco above the entrance of the library building of iron smelting,an industry Gosport had once enjoyed.As the bus slowed down I would climb down onto the rear platform,a steady hand from the conductress holding on to me,knowing that holding the upright chrome pole when it was slow enough, I would jump off before it stopped,running up the pavement next to the bus."You shouldn't do that" said Nana,accompanied by an"Oi" from the conductress as I stumbled off and sheepishly saying"sorry" I knew I would still do the same next time! Through the double doors at the library entrance I Approached the wooden desk where they would stamp the returning books I carried and return my tickets in exchange.Normally I would select new books from the shelves and repeat the process in reverse.Today,however, was different as we never selected any books, my ten shilling note in my pocket was going to purchase me a book of my own.We briskly walked down the High Street and entered the narrow door to Miles bookshop,next to the Evening News offices.I knew exactly the book I wanted and where to find it, it had a red dust jacket over a hard back cover and a little cameo drawing on the cover.Taking it to the lady to pay,I offered my note and received back a shiny sixpence in change.delighted with my purchase we finished our shopping and boarded the bus,complete with return tickets to return to Leesland Road.Removing the book from the shopping bag,before opening it I was made to cover it in neatly folded stiff brown paper to "protect it from finger marks",an   effective way to protect such a cherished item.

So effective,in fact, that sixty years later I still have that book and now read it to my two grandsons!!..What's the book?

"Winnie the Pooh by A.A. Milne

++

The summer school holidays loomed closer and sunshine under blue balmy cloudless skies heralded the prospect of no studies ,days of idle laziness bathing in the natural world.As the school term closed one of the final events was sports day,all of us wanting to take part in every race,and all of us wanting to win.Win,what,was not important,but winning definitely was,competition was very hot. It didn't matter whether it was egg and spoon,obstacle,wheelbarrow,three-legged,sack or the hundred yards race,if you won, you basked in the adulation of your peers,after all just taking part achieved little,life was always about winners and losers,success or failure.

The final tasks performed,school "broke up" and six weeks of lazy abandonment lay before us,very few were lucky enough to go away for a holiday,there wasn't much money, but lots of days in Privet Park,at Stokes Bay, in Lee on Solent or just down the old outdoor Gosport swimming pool was sufficient to enjoy at our leisure.

Days spent in "the park" lazily watching tennis or cricket in the afternoon's heat Even in summer the football always would accompany us in case we wanted a game,regardless of the heat, when we became bored watching the slow paced summer pursuits.Tennis players,always dressed in white,using white[no other colour] tennis balls and serving them with wooden Slazenger or Dunlop rackets strung with "catgut" and put to bed in wooden racket presses when finished with..The cricketers,also dressed in customary white,with the statutory jumper and coloured cap,which were regularly discarded, played out their game with heavy,rubber gripped bats and red shiny balls,mostly well worn and shared by all.Heavy white pads strapped on with leather traps and brass buckles and heavy laced boots cleaned with Meltonian shoe whitener completed the outfit.

The little pavilion in front of the Gosport Borough F C pitch served the teas to the hungry players,neat sandwiches,iced fairy cakes and an urn of hot tea.From the little window at the side we might get lucky and a penny would buy a cylindrical fruit ice lolly or a few "blackjacks" and three pence an ice cream cone....not soft ice cream but a slice cut from a long bar and pushed into a square cone with greaseproof paper! The luckier children,in which I include myself, were fortunate to enjoy these times,but as Dad was able to afford a car we had the extra treat of a holiday away.

++

 Cars were still fairly aged in their appearance and only just getting more modern lines,very different from today's sleek precision machines capable of what were then unrealistic speeds.Preparing to go on holiday by car was an adventure all of its own.
 Everything had to be checked,the leather seats polished,the paint and chrome polished,light bulbs and battery checked and replaced and topped up if necessary.Spark plugs and distributor were checked over as it was a real chore to start the motor with a starting handle,it was not enjoyable cranking the engine with the hope that it would fire up in a downpour.A heavy metal shaped bar was inserted through a hole in the cars front bumper.Once in it was engaged with the engine and turned as quickly as possible to fire the motor.The unwary,failing to get their hands away when it fired up could get a rap across the knuckles and even a broken finger from the moving handle.Tyres were checked for damage and a final wipe over of the wheels,some of which were wire spoked and tyres white walled was the final thing before setting off to fill with petrol at the garage.
 On arrival at the petrol pumps,tall metal cylinders with illuminated glass globes on top advertising Shell,Castrol.Mobil or National held a single black hose.The attendant[no self service] would come to the pump use a small handle to turn the pump to zero and then dispense the leaded fuel,no unleaded at these times,into the tank from which he had unscrewed the chrome filler cap.Refuelled, he would wipe the windscreen,check the oil and retreat into a small kiosk with the money, returning with any change due.At last with the final check on the air in

the tyres[cross ply,no radials,containing inner tubes] we were ready to travel....and the air was free!!

++

  In the corner of the small cold and gloomy bedroom lurked a faint shadow attached to a small boy who it followed endlessly.Ice patterns,like fronds of fern adorned the inside of the window panes and from the double iron bedstead a masculine figure was just awaking.The shadow watched intently as he began to move having been,woken by a clockwork alarm clock that was to blame for his arousal with its tinny jangling.The room was icy cold it's only insulation being the heavy blackout curtains hanging at the windows,left over from war years.No radiators,no fires,the only semblance of heat provided by the flame from the now flickering candlestick.The shadow faded in the light but the small boy remained there, and as the man washed in the cold water poured into a large bowl from a ewer he shivered at the thought of the chill.Briskly the man dried himself before proceeding to shave,lathering soap from a mug with a badger bristle brush and then scraping the lather and stubble off with a cut throat razor.

  Ablutions complete the man,himself,still shivering,pulled on his working clothes,bent and leaned under the bed,pulling out a plain white chamber pot,its contents being the nights human waste.He carefully carried it down stairs,closely followed by the little companion,which floated along behind him.As quickly as possible he passed through the back door in the scullery,before entering the outside closet and disposing of the chamber pot contents,bringing the pot back to "rinse out" before returning it to its place under the bed.Returning down stairs he went to the scullery,lit the gas stove with a match,filled a tin kettle and placed it on a gas ring.There was no electric kettles and no automatic power from the flick of a switch.The candle which had accompanied the man downstairs was now placed on the dining table and taking a spill from a jar on the mantle shelf he reached up and pulled a tiny chain attached to a light on the ceiling.The chain regulated the gas flow enabling the very delicate mantle to be lit through the hole in the base of the glass globe, hopefully without breaking it.

 As new light flooded into the room it was time to provide warmth and with no electricity supply the tiny hearth with a brass fender would need to be lit.A supply of wood and coal,accompanied by yesterdays" News Chronicle" provided the fuel source and until the fire was burning the cold would prevail.All this time the faint shadow and its owner accompanied the man,returning now to the boiling and whistling kettle.Removing the kettle from the heat a small drop of hot water was poured into the teapot,swirled around briskly then poured down the sink.Once the pot was warmed loose tea[no bags!] consisting of "one teaspoon per person and one for the pot"was placed in it before boiling water was added.The lid was put on,covered with a hand knitted woollen tea cosy and the tea "left to draw" before being poured.A glass pint bottle of milk was recovered from a bucket of water where it had been kept cool,no refrigerators,]pouring some into a little jug which was added to the tea tray.the remainder was poured into a saucepan and the empty bottle rinsed out.before placing it on the doorstep for collection by the milkman on his next round,Every morning porridge would be made from the basic ingredients,no instant ready made packets,] but nearly always Quaker Oats or Scotts.added to the milk in the saucepan and brought to the boil.The piping hot bowls,steam curling from the surface were carried on to the table and "sweetened"normally with a small amount of sugar,but the man preferred salt!...as a very special treat it might have Fussell's condensed milk added.

 The man took a crusty loaf of bread [no ready sliced items] from a white enamel bread bin, then a long knife with serrated edge,and placed both on a wooden board to carry to the table.If toast was required a slice cut from the loaf was threaded onto a long handled wire fork, held over the now blazing fire until both sides were brown,or even quite black and in need of being scraped, before spreading with yellow butter.No toasters and no dishwashers.Back in the scullery the kettle was boiled once more, the enamel bowl filled and the washing up began.Once rinsed of residual soap and soda crystals,having dried the utensils with a tea towel, "Best wishes from the Isle of Wight" printed on it, everything was returned to its rightful place in readiness for the next meal time.

 Grandad did it really take that long to get up in the morning?...did you go to work? I asked.

"Yes it did" It was all we knew,he replied,we were happy with our lives,we liked our daily routines. It was simpler but more satisfying than the constant stress that progress has managed to provide to so many people!

++

 Every moment,even those that seemed innocuous at the time,meant something.From the time we arrived.till the time somewhere in the future when we leave has provided a memory,many of which we will forget but some if we plan carefully we will pass on as a legacy to our heirs.

 I am fortunate to have a chance to recall these events be happy or sad,but I believe that it has given everyone the opportunity to dig into their minds and recall times which they may have experienced but have simply mislaid.

++

In 1954 I entered primary school at Leesland.a small Church of England school in an imposing red brick edifice completely surrounded by a playground of grey tarmac,which in turn was completely surrounded by spiked black cast iron railings.The surface sported small pieces of grit which invaded the cuts and grazes when you stumbled and fell...brushed away with your hand,spitting on the same to clean them,all forgotten in a moment.The playground on the Whitworth Road side regaled the area with three or four tall horse chestnut trees,a continuation of the lime trees which bordered the entire length of Gordon Road,until it joined Whitworth Road.

 The horse chestnuts provided numerous conkers,many obtained by the launching of objects into their laden boughs at autumntime to provide schoolboy entertainment.but this practice, for me,was to soon end.

 In 1961 March,my life changed once again.The eleven plus had been navigated by all my classmates but for me there was another challenging obstacle,one which would change my life forever.

 Dad had remarried soon after mum died but my bonds with Nana were as strong as ever especially at such a challenging time It was a damp cold day and suddenly another sibling entered the world and to make it more difficult I was to take an entrance exam to a school where my current pals were not attending.Needless to say when July came the close ties I had had with childhood school friends became more elastic,in some cases broken forever, I was to go to grammar school with unknown future classmates.September brought adventures in uncharted waters,almost literally as I now had to cross the sea on a daily basis,and Christmas 1961 was to bring a welcome respite.

 The nearby lime trees in Gordon Road provided aptly described lime green foliage as spring arrived,a touch of colour to an otherwise barren ribbon of granite.It was however one of these beautiful lime trees,aforementioned, that provided me with an unexpected memory,just a year later.

++

Outside the little sweet shop opposite the old Central School it produced a most unusual memory starting at midnight on Boxing Day in 1962.Nana had travelled home by taxi from my uncles party which had been at his house in The Haven at Clayhall,but I was allowed to stay later and could now be found walking,in fact running, home in the dark.Flurries of snow had graced the days approaching Christmas,but as I made my way home it started to snow in earnest and I recall the magic of the tiny flakes becoming larger as they blew into my face,obscuring my view as I ran.As I passed the trees,brushing against them as I ran on the ever slippier pavement,the snow falling on the hard frozen crust of the previous falls,there came a hollow thud and on peering back into the eerie gloom I sensed a figure on the ground which hadn't been there before,but who presumably must have been leant against one of the trees.The event has haunted me ever since...was the person unharmed...did they get back up..hopefully they recovered enough to make their completed journey.I didn't have the temerity to return to see,I was frightened of the dark and certainly of the possible person now laying in the falling snow which would soon be covering them.Leesland Road eventually appeared and hurriedly letting myself in I waited for tomorrow and what might befall.

++

It was not unusual for the morning to start out wet,but it normally cleared up by mid morning,so whilst waiting for fine weather and the chance to play outside the ensuing hour or two was passed entombed in the garage using the time as productively as was possible.Now,unfortunately, I found myself wet,muddy and very uncomfortable...behind me a misty yellow glow,above me pin points of light and a morbid feeling of maybe never seeing home again.When the weather cleared mid-morning it had been a case of get on my bicycle and pedal furiously to try to make record time from Rowner Lane to Privet Park.On my arrival,suitably exhausted,I met up with several friends,apparently in no fit state to play football but youth had no such barriers,appearances deceptive,two teams were picked and away we went.We could play forever and that was exactly what we did.Keeping an eye on more gathering storm clouds,as the sky reddened and dusk approached, we played on till we had drained the last drop of useable daylight.When the ball was no longer visible,the first large drops of rain falling and the breeze stiffening we said tired farewells and headed to our homes.

 The quickest route for me,I had the furthest to travel,was up Privet Road,turning right into Military Road and then came the first of three choices.Number one was to turn left and ride over an uneven muddy track around the perimeter fence of the old Grange Airfield.Number two was to traverse a narrower but just as muddy path along the railway line between Brockhurst Road level crossing and ending with a climb up the bank beside Rowner Arch.Number three was to ride on to Brockhurst Road at the junction adjacent to The Wheatsheaf public house,turn left towards Fareham and then take a left turn into Rowner Road.

 By now the rain was falling steadily and with the driving wind I had relinquished all rights to remain dry in any way..The last option was my favoured choice,so my journey found me pedalling along the poorly lit

Rowner Road, which in those days was narrow,dark.had no pavements and was edged with overgrown,weed strewn grass verges..in fact it was little more than a country lane!.After considerable effort I broached the summit of Rowner Arch before starting to coast down the other side on the last leg home,which leads me to the circumstances I now found myself in.Head down,not looking ahead I missed the flickering glow of the red paraffin road warning lamps and decided it was a great option to ride down a trench which had been dug .and which I was meant to ride around.As I lay on my back, watching the odd star through the scurrying clouds,my nostrils filled with the pungent odour of spilt paraffin oil.I was trying to decide which part hurt most,and hoping that

the no seven bus that had just topped the arch would have better judgement than me and not decide to join me in the bottom of the muddy trench.Fortunately the driver was more accurate than I and circumvented the hole in the road.progressing on his way which gave me time to climb back onto the road hauling my cycle with me.
 Unsure which part was most painful and having little stomach to rejoin the saddle I opted to limp slowly homeward,not sure if I was going to arrive.Of course there were no cycle helmets in those days in fact even motorcyclists were not made to wear helmets,so what seemed hours later I dragged myself through the iron gates at the end of our drive,on through a similar gate into the back garden and abandoned my transport outside the garage door.Opening the door to the conservatory before entering the kitchen where the figure standing there said "your late you've got paint on your face didn't you wash before you went out".I mumbled I know not what and slipped by and disappeared into the bathroom to survey myself in the mirror.
Blood had run from a cut on my head ,not red paint from the kiddies trike I had been painting that morning,drying on my face,there was a hole in my trouser leg and bruises were starting to darken ominously on various body parts.
 Cleaned up I didn't appear too bad and of course it soon healed,but I have one lasting "scar"to this day.Thirty years later I presented myself in an accident and emergency department with an injured knee requiring an x-ray.When complete the x-ray was being examined by a doctor who said "that break in your leg healed very well when did that happen".I had at that point never been to hospital in my life and said so, to which he replied that it must have been a long while ago as it was an old break The only thing I could think of was it had to have been that fateful wet night all those many years ago.

++

There was a sense of togetherness as there were so many families recovering from the tragedies of the war years,coming to term with the losses endured.I never thought to question why Aunt Ada and others had no spouse,it seemed normal, can't remember seeing a Mr Smith to partner Aunt Amy and certainly it wouldn't have been seemly to ask.All the family lived certainly within walking distance and very little distance from their birth homes,constantly keeping in touch with one another.However as well as the sisters there were,oddly enough, brothers who were never mentioned but for what reason we knew not and it would be deemed precocious to ask..Nana, by the end of the 1950's had seen the tragic loss of a son to tuberculosis,a daughter who had failed to survive a pioneering operation,and a loving husband who had just grown old and ran out of time.In spite of this she always found a reason to make time for her family members who were as she saw it,less fortunate than her.

Every evening she would walk up Leesland Road and visit her sister Ada who had sadly developed Parkinson's Disease.On times when I accompanied her we would sit and watch "Coronation Street" with Uncle Bert who welcomed us with a cup of tea and provided a biscuit to eat with it.

Aunt Ada laid propped up on a large bed in what would have been the living room,she was a frail lady with neat grey hair and glasses.Her head was always slightly bent but she never failed to muster a smile of greeting when we arrived,it never occurred to me how frustrating it must have been for her to be in her locked in world.

Another aunt we would visit every Saturday morning when we went to the butchers,she too was unwell and suffered from what today would be termed as mental illness.Auntie Flo's husband Will Le Ber was a tall portly gent with a round,ruddy,smiling face and best described as "Mr Pickwick with white curly hair",in sharp contrast to his ill wife.

++

Every week Nana would perform the same rituals but I remember in the early 1960's after Grandad Charlie had passed away her normal sprightliness became replaced with a certain weariness. A hollowness haunted her normally sparkling eyes and soon she fell ill and was admitted to Gosport War Memorial Hospital.

Hospitals and operations were certainly not like they are now and treatments were constantly being developed.An operation was necessary and once performed she returned to Leesland Road. Recovery was slow,healing even slower,the smile on her face forced,the twinkle in her eye always clouded.she never regained her infectious effervescence and began to deteriorate.Entering her normally sweet home,the normal lavender scent was replaced by an insidious odour which began to pervade the very fabric of the house.Despite visits from matronly nurses she slowly became weaker and eventually was transported to Dad's home in Rowner.The pain had become almost unbearable and in spite of medication and care the decline continued and began to affect her memory with the onset of a form of dementia.It was during this time that I entered her room and the contents of her handbag was spread over the ruffled bed covers.I started to put them back into the bag when she suddenly awoke and immediately accused me of stealing her money.Upset I left the bedroom and not long after she was admitted to Queen Alexandra Hospital,where I visited her for the last time.

As the years have passed the events have always stayed in my mind, and these early experiences of cancer and dementia had a profound effect on my development.What ignorance we met with in those early years has been replaced by better understanding and care.More progress needs to be made but the lasting recollection to these events was how primitive the treatments were and how misunderstood dementia was.People with dementia are not the person you remember but it certainly is not their fault.

The one question that I still have no answer for, however. is why such a pious, God fearing little old lady who embraced the sanctity of her beliefs so completely could have had to endure such physical and mental torment at the end of such a hard but generous life.

++

I want one of those......well you'll have to save your pocket money.....that seemed fair but if your pocket money, if you were lucky and actually received any, was one or two pennies a week, it was a monumental task to ever save enough for any coveted purchase..Money, maybe a half a crown or five bob from birthday or Christmas or a tanner from a visiting relative at holiday time helped augment the frugal stipend. For most however many wishes remained just a dream and it would be many years later that there was any fulfilment to many schoolboy dreams.
 So what did I do....either I had to lower my sights, give up or hire out my labour to achieve what was often seemingly almost impossible. Running errands, helping around the local shop anything to earn a penny, but with money scarce it was a hard day's toil to earn a very small reward.
 Children left school at fourteen years old and not long after, elder male siblings would be "doing National Service". Since 1948 on your seventeenth birthday you would be conscripted for eighteen months, into one of the armed services. On one hand it meant that there was a useful occupation at a time when unemployment was low, but it would provide training for conscripts to gain a worthwhile trade with which to attack the world.
 Whilst waiting for all these things to happen nearly everyone had taken up a hobby and inevitably many of those hobbies involved collecting things. Of course hobbies could be many and very varied, philatelist, numismatist, words which were elaborate for simple stamp or coin collector made it sound "posh".

Others had simpler pastimes which could be just as exciting and varied, building dens, climbing trees and generally exploring and discovering ......really the ideal environment for learning and appreciating the simplest things in life. Even the simple hobby of collecting things was governed by the lack of pennies. Nobody had collections worth huge amounts in value but often they consisted of items which to us were priceless and their value immeasurable. Not for us silver and gold, but what delight we got from what in many cases now would just be junk. We would start with collections consisting of simply rubbish, stuff we would normally throw away, of no further use, maybe cheese or fruit labels, bottle-tops, matchbox labels, cigarette cards, buttons, and even empty cigarette packets!! We would then progress to stamps, nearly always used, and postcards and foreign coins. All the time these items provided knowledge to the young receptive minds....if you were missing one you would "swap" with a pal who had a spare one to complete the set with.

Nature in turn provided more great opportunities, although with hindsight it was rather cruel and destructive. Collections of bird's eggs, butterflies skewered with pins, pressed flowers and even bird's feathers were all part of our informal education. Reflecting now I am able to see the qualities that this simple lifestyle instilled into me as an inquisitive person with a thirst for knowledge. Appreciation, patience, sharing, compassion, respect, humility.. ......all provided in what was around me.

+++

How confusing things could appear to a six year old just learning the skills of life, even more so when a conversation which went "well I don't think I want another one" was countered with " well I need about a dozen" was overheard. Strangely enough these obtuse dialogues often seemed to stem from supposedly wise grown ups, Dad and Grandad.

Most afternoons Grandad after his nap would don his flat cap,pull on his old grey jacket and with a "see you at teatime" would amble off up Leesland Road.Turning right when he reached the end, he would walk to the left of Ann's Hill Arch and join Middlecroft Lane.At the end stood the Middlecroft Arms,a grubby hostelry which always looked unwelcoming turning down the adjacent unmade track he sought the haven of his allotment and self made shed of salvaged timber.

The allotments stretched over a large area, all of them neat,tidy and immaculately manicured,regimental rows of seasonal vegetables,onions,cabbages,peas and broad beans,fruit bushes stood as a fence between the bursts of colour [often Dahlias which were popular] providing cut flowers for home.Each little plot thirty yards square provided a welcome supply of fresh food for the table and supplemented the weekly income which was about seven pound per week and pensions one pound thirty six pence a week!.These allotments had been tended during the"digging for victory" campaign during wartime and continued to be a source of healthy food.On arriving at the wooden shed made mostly from scrap Grandad would enter,remove his jacket,roll up his sleeves and change his polished shoes for sturdy boots.Suitably clad he would select his armoury to fight the engagements of the land.It might be old lace curtains to cover the fruiting berries,it might be a string of silver milk bottle tops which he used as bird scarers or just a simple armful of tools.There were various wooden handled hoes,forks,rakes,spades and the never to be forgotten dibber.This instrument,home engineered,to met looked like a sharpened broken spade handle and it was,recycled from the old when a new one had been fitted to a spade.Now,it was an essential piece of equipment for making holes to plant the ready to plant seedlings into and getting them in straight rows .One thing however never left the shed....a silk parachute canopy,or at least the remains of one, that had lain there since it was retrieved from the allotments during the war years! Its use I never discovered,nor where it eventually would go when Grandad was no longer able to tend his little patch.

Ready for work,the preparation almost as long as the task in hand,he would spend the next hours tilling the fine,stone free soil,hoeing,weeding,digging,planting and tidying between the various rows.He might stop to puff on his roll up cigarette as he returned to the shed to plant some seeds into wooden trays filled with fine sieved soil.The seeds he took from brown paper bags Which had been stored in glass jars,saved from last year's crop.Seeds weren't purchased each year but saved from year to year and were only replaced if the crop had been poor.

As teatime approached his last act was to collect some produce for the table at home,maybe a root of potatoes,some onions from the string drying in the shed,a punnet of strawberries or a few pods of peas,one of my favourites.The only problem was when I opened the pod there was the odd maggot or two, not really surprising as we relied on natural predators, not chemicals, to solve any aphid issues,something which was a small price to pay for a delicious harvest,and could well be adopted again today!

Trug of goodies in hand Grandad would go through a gate at the side of his allotment and enter a garden to a pebble dashed bungalow....16 Oxford Road....where I officially resided!! This was where the earlier mentioned conversation had taken place.Dad used to keep cage birds,of which I will talk of another time, and the word "perch" came up....the confusion was between the perches in the cages and the old traditional measurement of rods,poles and perches which were used to measure allotment areas till about 1965!! My thoughts of lots of little birds huddled together on a little stick still makes me chuckle today,but not as much as the vision of my Grandad digging not for victory but half of Gosport!

++

I neglected to tell you that I too was there
I neglected to tell you I thought you'd not care
I feel now I should have but now it's too late
But please ask the others that wait at the gate.

For me it is over now gone from my head
I now rest in peace along those that lie dead
I can't tell you now,for I'm no longer there
I wish that I'd realised that you did really care

Before we're all gone you must gather their thoughts
The triumphs and losses the battles they fought
Write down the memories the thoughts that they had
Recorded for all be they happy or sad.

Soon the'll be gone you can ask them no more
Before it's too late and the final encore
Life was too private,it was felt wrong to tell
Now almost gone we must hear of their hell.

The many that lived and the many that died
The times that they laughed and the time that they cried
The memories they forged in the thick acrid smoke
The young vibrant heros that never awoke

I am telling you this before it's too late
Tell what you remember and clearly to state
Memories are goldust and rich thoughts for all
So don't seal them in or else they will fall

++

As I wandered watching people everyday I remember that encompassed in our freedom and lifestyle,as a post war child, I was devoid of all memories of the not so distant conflict. I had no experience of what had unfolded for six years of many peoples lives....I thought they had only the happy carefree life that I was enjoying,not realising that the memories they had formed were not so joyous as mine but far more harrowing and haunting,I often wondered why certain things occurred...the little nuances,odd phrases,vacant looks often accompanied by"a penny for them '".The times when people were silently alone recalling their individual memories and thinking of the times and events they no longer wanted to remember.After all it is not easy to forget memories,good or bad,they simply fade as the years pass,they never leave us completely.Recalling these times there were instances when questions were posed but rarely answered,brushed away by"you don't want to know that" when really I did but was too scared to pursue..Alien iron ware and concretions were brushed off by the answer"oh it was something to do with the war" and I remember one occasion on seeing a neighbour on her own saying "why is there no Mr ?"...not realising they had been widowed.We walked past derelict piles of rubble and even played on them unaware of the adults memories of past residents.It was simply "Mrs ? and her little boy lived there,she was a lovely lady"

Today we have some idea of what may have been behind those comments,at the time they were meaningless and we paid little heed to them.These were other's memories very rarely talked about and belied by "the stiff upper lip".The camaraderie of the workers spilling out of the factories and dockyard stemmed from that tight sense of comradeship and togetherness bred in the war.

++

On one D-Day, as a child I have a lasting memory of my own that stemmed from that June event in 1944. On one our walks along Stokes Bay I asked, as we had on many previous walks, about the concrete pieces laid at the water's edge. Nana was in her late 70's and as she looked out sadly towards the Solent I heard her wistfully say "and they were so young they had their lives before them"

I can only surmise that her memory had returned to that beach in 1944 as wave after wave of hero's left to meet a future they knew nothing of. As they left fearlessly, smiling, hopeful of a triumphant return, for many Stokes Bay Gosport was the last British soil they would ever stand on. These memories had been locked in her mind forever, never to be forgotten, along with the sadness she had witnessed.

I cannot remember....I can only imagine....I can only reconcile what I saw with what might have been the reason..

She paused mid sentence and stopped pouring the tea...she glanced to a fading sepia photo on the mantelpiece and a misty glaze covered her eyes, a tear in the corner as she painfully remembered. It had been ten years but it may just as well have been yesterday and even when she left the two up, two down in Leesland Road the memory never faded, reminders still stood on many corners.

I remember her well as I do the others that daily walked the street, rarely smiling, vacant eyes hiding the pain, life was unforgiving..As I wandered down the street, little back gardens hid the corrugated iron shelters that lay underground before I arrived at a break in the Victorian terrace. Here was a pile of bricks, glass, wood fragments and mortar dust gradually being taken back by nature...the purple, yellow and white flora slowly mellowing the stark backdrop and bringing life back to the open space. An old man would sometimes stop whilst we played there, bowed head in thought, weakly smiling at us noisily chattering and as we found out later remembering the people that had had their lives abruptly ended where we now played.

He would turn away and momentarily pause, consternation in his eyes as the factory siren at Ashley's wallpaper factory heralded lunch break...then slowly walk back home remembering it thankfully was in the past.this time it wasn't an air raid warning..Going further into Gosport more reminders and evidence of a time of turmoil appeared,the large wild pitted area outside St John's church in Forton Road,the roofless railway station where passenger trains ran no more into the Victorian station that was Gosport.

Down to Spring Garden Lane into Walpole Road and before you reached the High Street you stumbled across the still damaged Holy Trinity church,weeds growing from the gaps where wind blown seeds had germinated.It was another reminder which you left behind you as you cut through South Street towards Pneumonia Bridge..the platform from which I was told the skies had lit up and skyline burned like a raging inferno that bleak,dark period of the past.Wending my way towards Gilkicker there lay on the ground rusting tin and scraps of iron,to us just metal but to the old lady and man constant wartime reminders.The old army command centre stood empty and as we walked past various towers ,concrete slabs came into view and at low tide a square patterned roadway led into the sea...the path to no return for many who left here in the previous decade.

At home again life to me was normal...it didn't occur then that when Grandad put his sugar in his tea sparingly it brought back memories of austerity.I walked past these things daily,I was oblivious to the poignant headstones in the neat cemetery that signalled the service and civilian lives that had been lost in that all encompassing conflict.

I thankfully was not there....I remember memories which when they were made had no significance...the widows with no husbands,the man with no family...now at a time we remember so many peoples sacrifice at D-Day,I now understand those memories and they make sense at last, I'm just sad that those many years ago I never realised the anguish these people must have felt everyday.

++

We joined the traffic flow northwards,the semaphore arm on the car accompanied by the required hand signal through the car window advising of our intentions,we were on our way.Us kids peered out of the back window making sure we had left no litter on the ground and thus the seemingly endless journey was set to continue.The boredom was tangible but soon relieved by a small gold tin,the lid adorned by a still life picture of a varied fruit assortment.When opened, under a wax paper disc,perforated with pin pricks,there nestled various hard boiled fruit drops in a drift of what seemed to be icing sugar.We all partook and started on passing away the remaining hours in the most simple ways as we sucked merrily away on the acid fruit sweets.

 First we played I-spy,then spotting different car numbers.The yellow A.A. book,supplied to every member of the Automobile Association listed the two letters identifying where the car was registered and there would be"an ooh and aah" if we spotted one from Scotland or Ireland,all the time our destination ever edged closer.Over the railway crossing.with its manual gates at Bamber Bridge,we headed past Deepdale .[Preston North End F C] football ground opposite Moor Park,the journey was close to ending and were we glad.As well as being tired and slightly,well extremely bored,it highlighted the lack of radios in cars of that era allowing Dad to practice his choral skills...which were virtually non-existent.We had been serenaded variously with Camptown Races,Widecombe Fair.Ilkley Moor Bah Tat.It's A Long Way to Tipperary and Mademoiselle from Armentieres.....staunch popular survivors from wartime England.
With a final flourish we turned into a wide cobbled street with high granite kerbstones and an equally wide pavement.The houses were tall and their red brickwork stained with black soot,Each terraced house had a wide deep porch which was tiled in William Morris style patterned floor tiles and led to a large door surmounted by a stained glass fanlight.The door opened into a wide gloomy very high ceilinged

entrance hall...the occupants an elderly lady and man both of whom had seen better times.As they spoke the Irish accent was unmistakable.The short slightly stout lady dressed all in black her white hair pinned back into a bun smiled brightly belying any discomfort caused by the heavy caliper and boot adorning one leg...the legacy of polio at a young age.The man was thinly built and neatly attired, his face displaying a grey flecked dark moustache looking not dissimilar to a shaving brush and a Chaplin style hat perched on top of thinning slicked back grey hair.When he spoke the aroma of alcohol filled the air,an unfortunate result from his experiences in two wars and the Irish uprising he had witnessed in Birr when his fellow countrymen burnt the barracks located just outside Birr,at Crinkle..

  These two diminutive people were our other Nan and Grandad,it was their home, and we had visited every year since they had moved to Preston from Clarence Barracks in Gosport.They had lived there for a long time since the Royal Leinster Regiment was absorbed into the Royal Welch Fusiliers soon after Ireland's independence in 1922 and his final army posting was to Haydock Camp.

++

"Come along we'll be all day if you haven't got it now you'll have to go without it."Frantically grabbing the last toys and books we bundled ourselves into the car and were ready to "hit the road"make sure the gas is turned off,windows shut and the last thing that the door is shut" said the same voice.

  At last Dad joined us in the transport,suitcases were stowed in the boot,a wicker basket filled with sandwiches,tomatoes,cake and beverages stood between the children on the back seat and the driver,who had now joined the female front seat passenger, made himself comfortable in preparation for the interminably long journey..we were going on holiday...the same holiday we went on every year in August.

We left Leesland Road,waved goodbye to Gosport and scuttled through Fareham,"now we haven't forgotten anything,have we".muttered Nana...."well if we have it's too late" replied Dad as we started up the A34.towards Winchester,and the charmingly named Sutton Scotney for a journey which would take all day,encounter numerous stops and eventually arrive in Preston,our destination two hundred miles away.

Winchester,Abingdon,Newbury,Oxford,with its dreamy spires, and Bicester slowly came and went as did Beacon Hill and a nuclear research station at Harwell.Huge strange shaped cooling towers signposted the power stations along the route.at Didcot with white steam billowing into the blue sky.

The road itself was single carriageway,there were not enough cars yet for dual carriageway and motorways had still not arrived on the scene.A-roads were the pinnacle of excellence with their unmown wildflower verges giving rise to tall hay like grass and myriads of jewelled butterflies.At various places we would stop in overgrown,litter free,lay-byes [everyone took their rubbish home] and in the relative silence wild birds would attend in both profusion and variety.
Packed back into the car,the ritual of "have we got everything" was performed once again,as it was every time that we stopped,satisfied that we did we then pulled back out onto the road. Along the verge we passed mile markers,often large hewn stone slabs painted white with black letters showing the distance,in miles,between the towns on the route,every so often yellow and black A.A. boxes,clearly numbered and named,just in case you broke down, would appear at the roadside.Similarly you would be passed by a smart motorcyclist with motorbike and sidecar who would give you a snappy salute if you were displaying a chrome A.A. badge on your radiator.Elsewhere the yellow and black boxes had been replaced by the blue and white of the R.A.C..

Passing through Bicester we continued northwards to Stafford and Stone,we gasped at Warwick Castle as we passed,then gazed at the beautiful cathedral at Litchfield.
  By now we were getting tired and bored so the journey took another turn....but those memories must wait for another day.

++

  For some time probably up to the early 1960's we lived to a set of values that spilled over from wartime Britain,The proverbs and sayings,the old adages which we set our store by were gradually eroded...eroded by progress created by ourselves.It almost parallels the sense of responsibility that we valued then with the advances and freedoms that we had ten years later,much to my regret.A favourite saying from Nana was that "money was the root of all evil" and if she looked back on the world she had left behind she would justify that by the way she saw things changing.As more modern appliances became available she would deride"the keeping up with the Joneses" mentality giving rise to the appetite to need more money.She would have applauded the "make do and mend" and "a stitch in time"way of living,and she would have condemned the idea of people almost replacing their simple but rewarding lives with one of always wanting what the next person had.I was always encouraged to do my best,achieve more,but not by the way of a continuous drive for more and more money,"you cut your coat according to your cloth"..She would have seen this as a move away from her religious beliefs and the advent of people putting their greed before more important feelings.Family first became first but only when I have what I want.
  The advent of credit purchases,the renewing of items that could be repaired,following fashion when new clothes weren't really needed,the unwillingness of people to wait....the lack of patience.Transport meant the opportunity to go further afield to gain better rewarded employment and in doing so fragmented families around the globe.Families at the

same time seemed to feel less responsible for less fortunate members and gradually we made the care of family problems,the elderly, other peoples responsibility.Family values were eroded,the elderly and sick are no longer respected or valued and now more of a nuisance.We used to respect elderly and value their knowledge,we"loved our neighbours" picking them up if they needed help or support...now few people see their neighbours or rarely know them,and certainly fall short of offering help..Greetings to all as you walked down the street have been replaced with icy stares and alien looks,saying "Hello" to a child made you a pervert. Ambulances were used as were hospitals for real emergencies not just a grazed leg or simply falling over,antibiotics were a last resort not handed out willy-nilly.

++

 As you look back and reflect you remember how and why we remember our formative years....progress and technology have opened up a new world which has lost many of those values that made our community so close.It has created as many problems with its onslaught as solutions, looking back I can see how much damage that has done.We need to take these years and use them to help us solve the issues that now present themselves.The old adages were entombed in a lot of truth and can assist today as much as they did in our childhoods....."waste not want not".live and let live" "do as you would be done by","make do and mend", there are a lot worse off than you".....I could add many more but they all have that logical reasoning that we grew up with.

++

 As I crossed the doorstep there was a cast iron flap set in the pavement which you could lift up by inserting a key in the small hole in it,this housed the stop cock,a brass tap which would turn off the water supply to the house.When I was idle, or waiting for someone to play with,I would poke all kinds of debris down into the chamber inside,as Nana would say"the devil makes work for idle hands".No tarmac pavement but paving slabs with real cracks in between,which gave rise to various simple schoolboy entertainment.The commonly played game of hopscotch used these pavings and you could entertain yourself by walking to school ensuring you avoided stepping on the cracks.Kerbstones were heavy and often of granite and I would balance on them trying not to slip into the gutter. The same material was used for the road chippings secured by tar to the road surface which on very hot summer's days would melt and returning from school would stick to the soles of our sandals.

++

The roads had little traffic as cars were a luxury and the ambulances,fire engines and police cars rang bells to warn of their impending approach.The vehicles of this time were becoming more mass produced and some marques began to disappear.Some models became with different names almost the same as they were produced from the same "mould',the Austin 1100,Morris 1100,Riley Kestrel,Wolseley and MG 1100 were so similar only the trims being different.Many of these makes soon became defunct and the names almost forgotten forever.Lorry names like ERF.Foden and Commer slowly disappeared,swallowed up and discarded like rubbish

In these streets there was very little rubbish and what little there was disappeared under the bristle broom wielded by the road sweeper daily....most of the rubbish he removed into his hand drawn electric float was actually grit and not the flotsam of modern day life.Even Leesland Road had a road sweeper and housewives almost competed to keep their front pavement the cleanest in the road and would scrub it with a bristle broom and soapy water!!

Amazing that such mundane actions instigated the competition we so much are persuaded to turn our backs on in present times.
At school the pupils vied to get top marks in their times tables or spellings.At school sports day,yes,we did have sports days,we would want to win,to be the best at what we did.No matter what the race,egg and spoon,sack,three-legged and wheelbarrow we would want to win and even then your were being taught to work as part of a team....even if only a team of two.However much we would like for everyone to be of the same ability it will never happen as competition is what people need,one individual will always be better than another.Taking part was a prerequisite....maybe choice is now too free and ability to opt out makes people lazy and able to achieve goals with little or no effort.

++

Throughout the '50's life to children seemed to be idyllic,a time when you could play outdoors safely doing things that were just about enjoying oneself. Everything I and my friends performed was at would by today's measures be classed as slow...to us it was just the speed at which the world lived in an era when the most important resource was where you lived,the simple natural environment.Surprisingly everything got done but even stranger was that it was done on time,appointments buses and trains mostly were on time and nobody was in a hurry...it wasn't necessary.
 I find it very difficult to understand why now when we have so many labour saving devices why it takes so long to do things that are so simple.It would seem to me that the devices designed to save time and be more efficient have almost certainly added to the time of the job they were supposedly designed to shorten.
 The house is a good place to start as in the post war years there were very few appliances.For the hard working housewives,in their pinafores and head scarfs everything was manual work, kitchen aids were the

new fashion as gradually saving time became an obsession,but for what end.Hoovers replaced brooms and dustpans and brushes,,,blenders and mixers replaced the good old porcelain mixing bowl and wooden spoons.Meals from scratch became ready meals and consequently we needed even faster means to cook them...the microwave.The enamel bread bin became a plastic bag and we said goodbye to the elm breadboard,butter dish and bread knife as we became thick and thin sliced and foil wrapped and in time appeared in plastic tubs.Milk became cartonned and long life,glass bottles disappeared and so also did the regular milk rounds delivered to our doorstep.

Smart wooden cased mantel clocks became digital wall clocks so it was easier to tell the time.Cooks in the kitchen didn't time things they let the cooker do it for them.Washing machines saved labour and created effluent problems and tumble dryers almost sounded the death knell of the washing line pulled to the top by a pulley system.Electric can openers replaced the old fashioned hand ones,two slice electric toasters replaced the figure crouched beside the fire with a simple wire fork and electric kettles switching themselves off so we didn't have to understand what boiling water was!

Refrigerators and freezers meant we didn't have to worry about items spoiling but even that became too hard for us so we had to print labels with "use by" dates

Gradually, trades people became harder to find as we threw things away instead of repairing them,up until now we had all performed minor repairs "in house" and prolonged replacement as long as possible.

All of these time saving devices and gadgets needed to be funded so we saw the housewife became the working wife,who now worked even harder to earn the money to pay for the items she had acquired to save her time,but still had to do that work as well.

As we lost those skills,those of how to make items last,now when we did need a repair the tradesmen were no longer there so appointments

became more and more unreliable with long waits.....due to less tradesmen.
  Sadly the more mechanised we became the more we had to earn to provide the items we were led to believe"every home should have".We now have no time because we are headlessly lurching further into an abyss,never questioning why,but really its in order to perform tasks which didn't take that long in the first place.
  It doesn't make me content to think I have all these modern implements in the name of progress......in fact all this progress is the prime reason for much of the causes of our tenuous hold on
what is left of our planet!
  Even more we don't need to have the ability to count or spell and surely it won't be long before the need to think will be removed from us as commonsense runs out thanks to various controls placed on our lives!

++

  A diminutive figure stood on tip-toe on a low brick wall peering through a small window running with condensation.It was cold outside and the small person was wrapped up well in scarf and balaclava hat to stave of the chill air.Next to the panes was a brown painted door,slightly ajar but not open enough to peer in,in any case the cobweb housing a black spider hanging from the lintel was too much of a risk to run in.In the gloom of the interior stood a toiling figure, back to the window but deftly working with items from the table in front of them.Above the table, hanging from the wall was a tier of shelves on which were various metal and glass receptacles filled with indistinct but forbidding looking contents.In the corner on the floor a baited trap was laid and in the opposite corner a counterpart had already dispatched a careless rodent a slight trickle of blood running from its lifeless mouth.In another area swirls of steam rose from large pans disguising their contents with lids perched to one side as they bubbled on the old gas stove.

Turning their vision to the table you could discern various plants,some in bunches and laying amongst various menacing instruments viewed amongst a macabre assortment of items... an array of silver fish with lifeless eyes.a pig's head,chickens feet,kidneys,hearts,various liver and what looked,in the gloom,like a pile of cotton wool!! On the edge of the table were clamped two small metal machines with handles under which were piles of brown and green matter produced when the figure turned the handles from time to time.

The figure as it moved would make a sound between humming and sobbing from time to time accompanied by the dabbing of their eyes.

The smaller figure peering through the glass suddenly slipped and stumbled into the door thrusting it open....the figure inside laid down the knife amongst the onions on the table.....turned and said "come in.pick yourself up and you can give me a hand",so with a sheepish look I bashfully entered.Nana loved to cook,she had been in service before the first world war and had taken the chance to write in longhand into a little blue-green book the recipes the old cook had taught her.All the items on the shelves and table made up the ingredients of one of those recipes.

The glass and metal objects on the shelves were blancmange moulds [shaped like rabbits and castles] and heavy Kilner jars for preserving fruit,runner beans,and other items for use in the winter months

The boiling pots on the ancient gas stove contained bones and vegetables to produce the stock for various pies,stews and suet puddings.The bunches of leaves from the table were fresh herbs from the little back garden..sage,parsley and thyme that when added to breadcrumbs and the chopped onions produced tasty stuffing...mint waiting to be chopped was added to sugar and vinegar and you had delicious mint sauce.

The items clamped to the table were a Spong bean slicer and a meat mincer and amongst the various instruments was,a knife steel,rolling pin,potato peeler,cheese grater and lemon squeezer to name a few. The other "food" on the table were commonplace "treats" to me as the "waste not want not" adage when food was short continued well into the mid 1950's.The fish were sprats.cooked and eaten whole after being seasoned, coated in flour and fried,delicious with bread and butter.The pig's head would provide.brawn.bath chaps and pig's cheeks.The chicken feet scrubbed and put in the stew pot provided a snack to nibble for the very hungry.Kidneys were either braised or fried and even chopped to add to the cheap stewing steak and made into a suet steak and kidney pudding or pie.Hearts would be stuffed and braised,liver braised or fried and the white cotton wool.....tripe, which would often be stewed in milk with onions...ugh!.

The little room,dimly lit.was the old scullery.the tears from peeling the onions and I was the little figure,as you guessed,peering through the window standing on the little wall surrounding the back yard drain!

++

A woman's work was never done! ...in fact there was always much to do and regarding the household chores that was her domain..a fairly distinct line was drawn,the man provided for the family...the wife managed the home.

Even when times were hard and money tight the lady of the house would always provide the victuals and nuance to provide fuel for the families survival.The command centre for this exercise was a small whitewashed room with a cardinal red painted floor barely six foot square.What that little scullery contained would overwhelm a magician and the space in which to perform domestic and culinary magic was"too small to swing a cat".This tiny cool room would just as quickly change to a heated airless boiler house as it changed its use throughout the week.

It would take the auspices of a bakery,a kitchen.a laundry, and surprisingly a bathroom as the week progressed,but almost as equally surprising was the equipment for performing all of these tasks was contained in this tiny area.Reflecting back it was clear that the daily tasks were very closely connected to the various dinners that would be made daily from scratch ingredients.On Sunday [the Lord's day of rest] the most complex and substantial meal was produced....the roast.This meal provided the basis of sometimes the next four days meals,cold meat and bubble and squeak,shepherd's pie and stew and dumplings.The rest of the weeks dinners being sausages [sometimes liver] usually served with mash and onion gravy.fish and chips,the only takeaway of the week and ham egg and chips.

The furnishing in this frugal room contained all that was needed to provide a balanced household.As you entered it from the small lounge dining room there was on the left a grey vitreous enamel gas cooker on four legs.A simple oven and four primitive gas burners provided the cooking area and on it stood various bubbling cooking pots and the trusty whistling kettle.In the corner was the backdoor leading to the small shaded yard,home to the zinc and wood meat safe [our refrigerator of the time].To the right of the door was a white waist high Belfast sink.a zinc pail of water which the glass bottles of milk were kept cool in summer and then a lidded copper boiler.Hanging above it was a zinc bath next to a wooden,plywood larder and on the last wall was a set of wall shelves lined with wax paper beneath which was a bleached pine table, white from constant scrubbing.

Monday was washday when the copper would be boiling all morning,the washing dolly constantly pounding various items in the "tin"bath,occasionally a bar of red carbolic soap was added and the corrugated scrubbing board used to remove more persistent stains,its life as a skiffle board put on hold!

Tuesday the dry and clean washing now aired[having been removed from the wooden clothes horse by the open fire] was ironed on the aforesaid table before being neatly folded and put in the linen chest. Wednesday was a deep cleaning day,almost a mini spring clean, before we would go to visit my uncle,who lived in Clayhall, in the afternoon,Thursday was shopping day and Friday was spent preparing for the baths,an ordeal in itself as bathing in the large tin bath in winter was almost unbearable due to the cold.

  Saturday was preparing for Sunday with last minute shopping and the afternoon recreation was spent watching football or cricket.Time management had not been invented but Nana and fellow housewives had been doing it for years before it became fashionable.

++

  I awoke this morning with bright sunshine streaming through the curtains,wandered down stairs to the kitchen and realised there was a shadowy figure behind me.In fact there were three...a grey haired lady,a slightly taller man,and a child of about eight.
  I half turned and watched, following the old lady as she entered a small scullery where a tin kettle sat on the old well worn gas stove.She pulled a kind of wand from the stove,turned on the gas tap,clicked it,held it to the gas ring and the ensuing spark ignited the gas.That done she turned to a wooden door, shot a large bolt and clicked open the old fashioned door latch before exiting into a small backyard.She made her way to another latched door,entered and re-emerged a short time later accompanied by the sound of running water from an outside toilet.Gathering up her apron she went to a rickety shed, gathered a bundle of firewood then returned to the house.
  By now the elderly gent who was in the scullery had filled a tall floral patterned ewer with boiling water from the now whistling tin

kettle,turning away he carried the ewer ponderously up a wooden staircase and placed it on a marble washstand.Although the room was cold he stripped down to his "long johns" and started to have a brisk wash, before taking a badgers hair shaving brush,wetting it,lathering up the shaving soap and applying it to the stubble on his chin.He then took a cut throat razor,sharpened it on a leather strop and used it to remove the soap and stubble from his face.Taking a clean white towel he wiped himself dry and took a clean white shirt from the bed, putting it on before attaching a crisp starched collar with collar stud, he then fastened the cuffs with a pair of cufflinks that had seen better days.

Returning down stairs there was now a roaring fire and the house was beginning to warm up.Crouched by the fire was the child holding a long wire toasting fork which held a roughly hand cut slice of bread waiting for it to brown,although it had started to blacken around the edges.The elderly lady came in from the scullery carrying bowls of steaming porridge and took the slice of toast,buttered it whilst hot and placed another slice on the fork.By now the gentleman had joined them at the table,mugs of piping hot tea had appeared and breakfast was ready.The child was helped to a spoon of condensed milk on his bowl,the man added salt to his and the grey haired lady added a small amount of sugar.Grace was uttered and breakfast commenced in silence ,not a word spoken till all had finished.

The man then pulled on his coat,laced his highly polished shoes from the night before,perched his peaked flat cap firmly on his head and bid farewell as he left for work.The lady cleared the table,carried another jug of hot water upstairs to the wash stand and proceeded to help the child to have a good wash.On picking up the child's flannel shirt she noticed a missing button,but it was one of only two shirts and the other was still wet from wash day.Out came the button tin,a match was found and needle and cotton affected the urgent repair! Dressed with the now suitably improved shirt, hair brushed and neatly parted to one side the child was ready for school.The elderly lady quickly

dressed herself,covering her hair with an appropriate hair net,attached her bonnet with a lethal looking hatpin and at last everything was ready.
 A cry of "is the tea ready" awoke me from my daydream,no longer was I in 80 Leesland road in 1958,I was in my present home surrounded by toasters,electric kettle,hot water, microwave,blender and central heating in 1968,........but oddly I know even with all these new gadgets, in many ways I would rather be in the previous decade when.It was harder ...but it was happier.

++

 Last evening I was waiting for an event that has happened every year since I have lived in my present home where I have the benefit of no external artificial light.The reminders of those dark nights from Leesland Road and its tiny back garden and the little insects that dwelt in the grass.Darkness was deep and every May,cockchafer beetles or stag beetles had tapped on the window attracted to the lights inside as possibly they have done since 1885.....this year however there are none...possibly now extinguished by over use of chemicals in the never ending pursuit of food by the farmer to provide for an ever expanding population.
 Tinged with sadness I began to reminisce on other sounds and sights of nature which Gosport had in my childhood.....some still there but many becoming an ever rarer experience.
 From the weed strewn lawn dotted with trefoils,clovers,daisies buttercups [do you like butter was asked as the yellow flower was held under the chin] and the delicate dandelion seeds which we would blow"to tell the time",we have now created a sterile area of green sward, unable to support the life of hawk moth caterpillars and the incandescent glow worms,devoid of the chirruping cricket and its smaller compatriot the grasshopper.

The screech of the barn owl and twit twoo of the tawny owl are now heard rarely but in the '50's it was a common sound around the cemeteries and hedgerows.In the sky above the shrill twitters of the martins,swifts and swallows hunting insects on the wing and melodic sounds of ever ascending skylarks as they vanished from view high in the azure sky.

In the autumn sky skeins of cackling geese and the wing beats of majestic swans could be heard as they descended on the haven at Titchfield [long before the RSPB took over].A short distance from there you could hear the plop of water voles,the gribbit of frogs and the distinctive croak of the toad as they frolicked in the pools and ditches.In the cornfields opposite you would hear the rustling of stoats and weasels hunting for rabbits and mice and the clucks of corncrakes and partridges as a brown hare sprinted from its sett.

These sounds do exist but now you have to search for them...oh how relaxing it was to lay in the luxury of a sweet smelling clover meadow,enjoy the smell of new mown hay,and listen to the vibrant hum of thousands of tiny insect wings as lazy colourful butterflies meandered across the sky

Nature provided a constant education for us but the present rush of progress is only now realising just what an asset we still have but are in danger of losing.....and just how important it is to educate this generation about it before it is lost forever.

++

Thursday was always shopping day in Leesland Road and thus the days routine, as ever, was a carbon copy of the previous week.As daylight arrived the local cockerel crowed in the first light.Soon as you were awake you went downstairs where the wood in the fire crackled as it burnt accompanied by the spitting and little puffs of noise from the anthracite as it released its captive gases.

Outside to the privy with its own unique sound of the chain and iron sanitary furniture as you pulled the flush,your bottom smarting from the shiny Bronco toilet paper.As you left the wee house you could hear the breeze blowing the foil milk caps threaded on string as bird scarers,placed amongst a row or two of peas in the neighbours garden..

 Entering the scullery the whistling of the kettle, made as steam escaped from the cap enclosing the spout greeted my ears and the chink of cutlery and china added to it as breakfast was set.

On cue there was the strange hum of the hand propelled milk float as it stopped at every door,the bold whistle was often tuneless as the milkman clinked the glass bottles together and placed them on the doorstep,taking the empties with him.

 The breakfast consumed and doors opened and closed as the male incumbents left for work,summoned by the factory siren for the first time that day....the second and third times being at dinner time and the final signalling the end of the day.A little later Nana and I would leave for our shopping expedition into town accompanied by the harsh scrubbing sound of bristle brushes as doorsteps were impeccably cleaned.Onwards past St Faith's Church at the end of Tribe Road where today silent, the angelic treble voices only to be heard singing at the Sunday service,the bells rarely rung,.Down Harcourt Road and as you reached Whitworth Road if you looked to the left towards Lees Lane railway gates you could sometimes catch the shrill whistle,escaping steam and clanking wheels of the railway engine on its way to Gosport Station..Down at the corner of Vernon Road was a little sweet shop but today it was the opposite corner and into Mr Jones the butchers.Here you would hear the thud as the cod-fat was beaten flat before being rolled around the beef rolls for extra basting.Purchase made and time to pay,the tap of the till keys,ring of the bell as the till drawer opened with a quiet thud and then the chink of the coins falling into the till drawer followed by the sound of it closing.

 Continuing down Whitworth Road we entered Mills the cobblers where the door opened with the jingle of a warning bell above it, the staccato

tap of the hammer upon the last came from where a leather apron clad worker sat.
  The final leg of the journey was by omnibus.Once aboard the conductor or conductress rang the bell to give the all clear to the driver to move off,an action replicated at every bus stop.In between Whitworth Road and Gosport High Street.You were treated to the distinctive whirr of the ticket machine with a telephone style dial dispensing a permit to ride.as each passenger paid their fare.
  We arrived in the town and new sounds were all around to add to these and others.The delivery man with his call of "co-op",the man with his cry of "rag and bone"and the clip clop and whinney of the vegetable man's trusty steed.
  This was a memory of the sounds, most of them no longer readily heard, that was the background to a childhood in the 1950's.....

++

  Monday,the start of a new week and it was back to primary school...halcyon days of blue skies and white fluffy clouds...or cold gloomy wet winter days....either way they were the best of times Up in time for a breakfast of cereal,porridge or blackened,but tasty, toast fresh from the open coal fire,a drink of milky tea or just water then wash and dress for the day ahead.
  No designer clothes,no trainers and no fancy hairstyles....if you had asked me about these things you would have been given a quizzical look as at that time they were just imagination,like science fiction and futuristic imagination.We were dressed in clean neat respectable basic clothes and shoes,often showing wear and tear, and in many cases previous sibling use.Grey flannel or white shirts and a tie,buttons sewn on with the wrong colour cotton belying their age.A short sleeve pullover,or a long sleeved one in winter often darned and with leather patches on the elbows,short grey flannel trousers,sometimes with rather worn seats!.Socks,normally grey,long or short,the long ones held

up with elastic garters and shoes or sandals with brass buckles hiding the "spuds" in the sock toes.

The belted mackintosh worn when raining in the winter was made of gabardine, rubber boots and sou'wester hat completed the outfit.by contrast in summer,maybe,a camel coloured duffle coat,open toed sandals and a rather embarrassing white cotton sun hat.

To complete the outfit a pull tie shoe bag made often of old curtain material or if you were lucky a small brown satchel with brass buckles.In these bags would be the little books with the words and tables you had learnt that weekend.No calculators,no computers,iphones or electronic gadgets they were to be part of our future and in 1955 part of the unheard of.

Thus prepared we would skip to school accompanied by our adult companions,Most children lived close enough to walk to their school...no school run,no cars...most families couldn't afford a car let alone one for the wife as well,in fact more women than not couldn't drive...it was more a school walk!

Into the playground and an orderly queue was formed to enter the school building.once the bell rang you formed up in your classes and once settled and orderly you followed the teacher into school.

Coats were taken off and hung with your school bag on the hooks provided on a bar above low wooden settles in the changing room and then into class.On Mondays the whole school gathered in the hall in front of the stage for assembly where the headmaster,Mr Washington would lead the prayers and hymn.Every morning during the week a prayer was said in each class before the school register was taken,each pupils name was called and greeted with either silence or a shout of "present miss'.Mondays were also National Savings day when you could buy saving stamps[depicting Princess Anne or Prince Charles] to stick in a book that once full could be taken to the post office and deposited in a savings book..

Playtime would come,no grass, just tarmac surfaces and various activities would occupy our ten minutes,after we had drunk our third of a pint of milk,sometimes appetizingly cool in winter,other times revoltingly warm in summer,although in winter it depended on whether it had stood in front of the coal fire in the classroom.Five stones,jacks,marbles,in autumntime conkers,minus goggles,knocked from the playground trees by throwing up sticks or plimsolls accompanied by reprimands from the patrolling duty teacher.Occasionally a peashooter made from a hollow plant stem,a tin one from the toyshop too expensive, fuelled with dried peas, or a catapult made from a forked stick and powered by elastic,sometimes a garter, would appear and provide the undoing of its owner!

Other pupils would choose teams and play more energetic games,British bulldog,tag,and the more risky kiss chase,risky as it could end up with embarrassing rejection,or even simply relaxed hopscotch.

The morning break had seen those not drinking milk having a watery orange juice in a glass bottle with a green foil top.No Health and Safety...common sense dictated if the glass broke it would cut and sensibly somebody would "guard" any broken glass whilst another child would arrange the clearing up...we learnt to be responsible for our actions and how it might affect others.

What happened....a state created by us and our children where everything was thought out for people and less need to think for ourselves.....no need for commonsense,care or responsibility as others did it for you.

Home for dinner and the afternoon session we did it all over again...except the milk.

++

Well it's Sunday the car filled with fuel,the picnic in the boot and we are all firmly [no seat belts] in our seats and off we go.At a slow but steady speed we headed out via Rowner Road,which was nothing but a narrow road and in fact almost a lane in places,on our way to Stubbington where we passed the church and village green before going through Titchfield to join a main road.The main road the A27 was a "fast" two way route and in those days B, C even D roads were far more common place Once on the main road we travelled towards Southampton,over the old Itchen bridge through St Denys and down past the railway station,going over the bridge turning left and heading towards the New Forest.You went past the docks where there was often a view of one of the liners of the day,Queen Mary,Queen Elizabeth,United States or Mauretania.before rattling on towards one of several destinations.

 Normally we went over the railway at Lyndhurst Road bridge just down from the Angry Cheese Cafe as it was then,and headed towards a little gravel track into the forest.On the return journey we would sometimes call in for a cream tea treat,at the little cafe on very special occasions.

 The roads in the forest were completely unfenced and you could pull off down little tracks and find yourself in leafy glades with rickety wooden bridges over crystal clear streams.Wildflowers were in abundance and birdsong filled the air but then the number of people and cars was far less and the New Forest ponies far more in number. Our picnics was spread out on tartan travelling rugs and apart from sometimes annoying flies our only visitors were the ponies,cows and sometimes odd pigs turned out for pannage in the autumn.

 Sometimes this would be our final destination but other times would see us continue to the Rufus Stone,or onward towards Lyndhurst,where we would play ball games on the green, opposite the majestic Grand Hotel.Further still would see us at Bucklers Hard and the banks of the Beaulieu River.At the last destination there was always a large gathering of ponies with their foals and you could get quite close to them.It was here that my sister who was obsessed with horses almost lost her love for the four-footed equines when she bent over and one protective mare managed to kick her up the bottom.The journey home was rather fraught and tearful, but a visit to the tearooms at Lyndhurst on the way home and a vanilla ice cream cone managed to staunch the tears and extinguish the frown,giving the rest of us a little peace and quiet!

++

Memories are thoughts of long time ago
Recollections are thoughts that we need to know
What if they're forgotten because nobody tells
Then those memories dissolve along with ourselves

We now need our memories the older we grow
To help us look back and help us to show
To our kin that remain when we are long gone
The mistakes that we made and tell right from wrong.

The thoughts that we had in the time we grew older
Have made us both clever and very much bolder
To tell sons and daughters mistakes from the past
And show what to do to make our world last.

We have to return to the make do and mend
We have to re-use,recycle re-bend
The metal and wood that we throw away
Those items that would last, just one more day

We need to tell everyone what life was like
When we didn't all drive but used our fee or a bike
When children played happily out in the road
Ran in the field learnt of newts frog and toad

We need to use memories before they get lost
To lay down a plan our recollections tossed
To make all the changes.needed to survive
To pass on those memories whilst we're still alive

I have tried in my memories to help you share yours
I hope you are able to make your thoughts theirs
And pass to your children what they may never have known
What your childhood was like and how you have grown
....UP!

++

 Bit different memories were how we lived in the 1950;s by a lot of idioms.A few of these I have listed but I would like you to add to them some which help you to recall your own personal memories from the 1940's and 50's .Sayings like………..

Least said soonest mended

A stitch in time saves nine
Do as you would be done by
Pride comes before a fall
Look before you leap

I'm sure you will know many more but that's a start!! I really would like your help on this one in recalling your own memories!

++

Grandad was a quiet,dour gent always dressed in a customary cap and very much a creature of habit,probably inherited from his days of service in the Royal Navy.His little part time job,cleaning at Fosters the tailors on the corner of Bemisters Lane [later Burtons] was the main part of his daily routine.My memories of him sweeping the pavement outside the shop,polishing the brass letterbox when we went to town on Thursdays or often he would be outside washing the shop window, immaculately dressed in suit and tie stripped to his waistcoat out of the pocket of which hung a loop of silver an Albert chain..anchored in his pocket by a large hunter....wrist watches were still to replace these timepieces for the traditionalists.Crowning this of course was the flat cap and occasionally you could glimpse the red braces supporting the wide bottomed and neatly turned up breeches.

Accompanying the watch in his pocket was a battered silver cigarette case which had survived the first world war with him and also the episode up the apple tree in the second world war. An equally battered flip top cigarette lighter and a "couple of bob" made up the rest of his luggage

The remainder of his day was almost like clockwork, we could tell the time by his movements.He would arrive at The Junction on the corner of Whitworth Road and Leesland Road as the hostelry opened having ambled up at leisure from his daily chore.It was always a pint of bitter,one only,and then the walk up to no 80 Leesland Road. I would watch as he slowly stepped up the road until he reached Tribe Road at which point I would run down to Hornes shop at the corner of Norman Road to wait for him Even though traffic was minimal I was not allowed to cross over and I waited for him to cross to my side of the road where I could then hold his hand all the way home.Twelve thirty was dinner time so he arrived just in time to wash his hands along with us,sit at the table,and wait for Nan to present his food on a white plate.On occasions,when hungry he would start to pick up his knife and fork before Nana had settled to say "thanks to the Lord" and he would be sharply corrected with "Charlie! grace! where are your Manners"

Dinner complete he would make one of his cigarettes,rolled from tobacco in a brown pouch with Rizla red or green papers which also lived in the well worn pouch.He would flick his silver lighter into life and we would vie to blow it out rather than let him use the self-extinguishing mechanism....other times he would light a spill from the holder on the mantle above the fire..using the coals to ignite it.

He would sit in his old wooden armchair,"letting his dinner get down" reading the Daily Mirror, the few strands of wispy hair combed back like Bobby Charlton years later at the end of his football career.He would use a wooden toothpick to remove remnants of food from the gaps between his yellow nicotine stained teeth.All set he would then start to read,invariably this would end with delight on my part but consternation on his.

Relaxed and happily drawing on a cigarette held between almost brown fingers from the tar in the "roll up",I would watch his head gradually,slowly, bow and drop as sleep started to take over,the after dinner nap was important to him to recharge his batteries..

A lot quicker was the movement ,however, when shouts of "Charlie what do you think you're doing" jolted him from his slumber and frantic brushing down of trousers to extinguish the smouldering paper he sheepishly grumbled to himself.I often wondered what Nana made of the news when she later read the paper...complete with various charred holes!

++

I remember a warm summer's day in 1956,having seen a huge white tent erected in Brockhurst Field when Nana said we were to visit the tent,it could only mean a day at the circus but unusually she seemed very excited by the prospect,herself.The only big tents we had ever visited before had been in same places, normally Walpole Park or on one occasion on the green at Stokes Bay.There were always long queues as we waited with bated breath.It was off course normally that of Jimmy Chipperfield or Billy Smart held in a big colourful marquee with a huge central pole which to me reached to the sky.There were all sorts of animals [at that time we were enthralled to see such exotic beasts and were not aware of their plight] we wondered at elephants,lions,camels,horses dogs and even budgies.The laughter was provided by the slapstick of the clowns,the skill by the juggler,tightrope walker and the trapeze artists,All were controlled by the red coated ringmaster with his black top hat and long curled moustache armed with his characteristic whip to keep order.

The only other time we visited Walpole Park was to go to the fairground...and what a fairground it was.It teemed with various rides from children's merry go rounds to adults ferris wheels and the scary ghost trains,my favourite was the dodgems where the attendant skipped from car to car admonishing over exuberant individuals. whilst being showered with sparks from the rods making contact with the wire mesh canopy.Around and in between were children's delights,shooting ducks,fishing ducks from a play pool,coconut shy,hoopla and for the older fair goers the test of strength with the mallet and bell!! Prizes were mostly cheap...stuffed toys,goldfish peering at you from a circular fish bowl,chalk spaniels and chalk ducks or seagulls which later flew on the lounge wall at home.

However this afternoon we walked over Ann's Hill and joined the ever growing throng walking up Brockhurst Road.By the time we reached the junction with Military Road it was frantic and became even more so as the crowd swelled with people being dis-engorged by buses arriving at Brockhurst,there were too many people for a circus and they were too smartly attired.

There in Brockhurst Field,long before Brune Park School had ever been thought of,appeared the biggest white marquee I had ever seen.We filed through the entrance and made our way to the tent,Inside were rows of seats set in front of a lectern and hymns

boomed from several loudspeakers.
Why were we all here...to this day I am not really sure....but suddenly the music quieted with the arrival of the enigmatic figure of a tall,smiling man,curlyish hair neatly combed,shiny black shoes,grey suit and tie....speaking with a mellow but commanding American accent that demanded your attention.
 The audience were entranced by his enigmatic presence and held on to his every word hoping for spiritual guidance in their everyday lives.The man was the Evangelist...Billy Graham....preaching his own pious,religious message as how people should conduct their worldly lives....did the people agree or comprehend....possibly not!!

++

 Sunday...."For what we are about to receive may the Lord make us truly thankful"...those words will resound in many ears from my generation...but why? No meal would have been complete without grace.Very often it would have been unintelligible it was uttered so quickly, to enable you to get to your food first,or to acquire the "best" of what was on offer before anyone else.
 A reprimand of "God's watching you" from Nana reminded me of my manners and made me slide awkwardly back into my seat.When you did get to consume your victuals it was to be in silence,with closed mouth and no elbows on the table.You were asked on those rare occasions if there was enough for second helpings if you would like more,you didn't ask but you did ask to leave the table at the end of the meal when everyone else had finished theirs.
 At bedtime I knelt at the side of my bed and piously said my prayers before I jumped in with the heat from my red rubber hot water bottle.
 It wasn't anything unusual for the family to go to the cemetery at Ann's Hill and pay respect to departed loved ones,to tidy the graves and

refresh the flowers. In the old Victorian cemetery with its weathered headstones,surrounded by a wild tangle of ox-eye daisies knapweed and quaking grasses under yew and monkey puzzle trees the gravel paths meandered endlessly.To walk or clamber over gravestones was taboo as after all "that was someones final resting place"In the new part of the cemetery the graves were more recent and neat in rows,the white marble still unblemished by the ravages of inclement weather.On weekdays when special visits were made to mark birthdays or anniversaries you would see the gravedigger preparing a new grave.A small man dressed in brown trousers tucked in woolly socks,a white shirt ,sleeves rolled up and the required flat peaked cap of the day.At times he would lean on a pick or shovel as he had a rest and drew on a pipe and if he had finished.a green mat would be placed over the mounds of brown earth and wooden boards placed around the grave edge to protect mourners from the mud.
  It was all tranquil and peaceful,an area for reflection.If a funeral was taking place or even if a cortege passed you in the road everyone would stand in silence,hats off and bowed heads as a mark of respect, many making "the sign of the cross".The same respect paid by curtained windows when neighbours had passed on.
  Leesland C of E school would say prayers before the school day and

twice a year [Easter and Christmas] all the children walking in twos would head to their own Noah's Ark.....St Mary"s at Alverstoke.The journey down Gordon Road and along the leaf strewn Green Lane was made in an orderly and disciplined manner so as not to offend other members of the public,or"to let your parents down"
  It was not till I wrote this memory that I fully understood just how much religion had played in the way I am now.All through previous centuries people had a maxim from which to draw from....in our generation,probably the last,it was the church.I am unsure now that

technology and "progress" has developed with pace, what that mantra is now....or even if there is one.

I am not necessarily a religious person but can see that in that post war period it did provide the basis for a society that needed order and guidance after the turmoil of the recent war.

++

Forty years ago the doctors we have all spoken of with a certain reverence and respect,thought that they would have been remembered so long after their demise.At a time when coronavirus was the scourge of the world It says a great deal about the way they conducted themselves.You always saw the same doctor,unless on holiday,they would do home visits without question and the continuity existed because they knew you like family and happily listened to family issues.No coronavirus but polio,tuberculosis,diphtheria or scarlet fever certainly brought just as many problems and devastation.

You could arrive with no appointment,you were always seen and an emergency was an emergency, when the doctor had to leave the surgery, but the patients were happy to wait for his return,Safe in the knowledge he had gone to somebody worse off than you and you would be seen on his return.

As of nowadays we too had innocuous and persistent ailments and diseases but the minor problems [unlike now] did not necessitate a doctor visit and hospital attendance [unless an emergency] was by appointment only, common sense or home remedies mostly prevailed.Grannies old wives cures were as in the song"most efficacious in many ways"

At this post war time we were still in the final throes of tuberculosis,many still succumbed to its clutches, alongside this came chest infections and bronchial problems not helped by the conditions we lived in.Waking in the winter mornings was freezing cold with ice ferns on the inside of the windows,the rooms were draughty and damp [no double glazing,no central heating,no hot water on tap]often mould on the walls.When you arrived outside we were met with thick yellow sulphurous "smog" which invaded your lungs with every sharp intake of breath.

I remember every morning for years laying over a chair,head covered with a towel to inhale the steam from a bowl of hot water,then having my back heavily struck to relieve the congestion in my chest [one of the lucky ones]in order to dislodge the phlegm that had invaded my lungs during the night.

Young people could be seen wearing iron calipers to support the muscles wasted by polio before it was eventually eradicated.

Chicken pox,german measles,mumps and measles [I spent many days in a darkened front bedroom in Leesland Road recovering from the latter].Diphtheria and Scarlet Fever still spread their deadly webs but as we now know vaccines and antibiotics weren't far away.Now the vaccines are effective in many of our childhood illnesses,but overuse of those very same antibiotics may prove to be our undoing.

You see illness and mortality were in abundance unlike now the only real difference is that they spring a new one, on us as fast as we destroy the old ones.

Children and mothers were more likely to die at childbirth,life

expectancy was lower,survival from operations was rather hit or miss but the research performed was to reward the generations now,if only it had been the same in 1954 my life may have been very different and my memories would very likely have been quite different also,

I get great solace from the fact that my mothers operation in 1954 was one of only forty that had been undertaken ....four..yes just four survived.Now the survival rate is ninety eight percent and she would have been proud that she had helped so many by her sacrifice when there was only a ten percent chance that she would return alive and well.

Alighting from the bus on the corner of Harcourt Road and Whitworth Road we would go into the chemists shop.Here in the little pale green painted shop which was entered up a step or two,through a door which was set at an angle adjoining the two side walls and windows surmounted by leaded glass panels was housed a myriad of self efficacious medications.Every conceivable ready made remedy....be they good or bad but needless to say most have now been relegated to the rubbish bin by modern treatments.Here you could purchase the contents of the medicine cabinet of the time,the chemist stocked them all..

Certain items didn't need purchasing like the spittle you cleaned your cuts with if you fell and the strips of old white bed linen which acted as bandages! However you did need to buy the little cream circular tin scripted with the word "Germolene" containing the pink ointment which may be needed to go on the bandage.

Various other items would find their way from the chemist to the medicine chest.Borax crystals for fungal foot infections and purple potassium permanganate crystals which were used as an antiseptic.Another colourful additive was iodine which was liberally used on cuts.Witch hazel solution was available"to bring out the bruise".Kidney shaped green,red and white tins of Epsom Salts were taken for a healthy liver when dissolved in a glass of water.Senapods,oil of cloves,syrup of figs and wonderful concoctions like" Famel" and "Alka Seltzer" tablets helped you through the more minor ailments.

Then of course there were the tested traditional "old wives"remedies,...Beefsteak,beef tea,chicken soup,mustard powder[for tired feet] and bread poultices all supposedly healed you in some way,but sometimes were just imagination.One of the popular brands was the 'Steradent' tablets put in a glass beaker containing Nana's dentures to clean overnight,but which would mysteriously get mislaid.Lucky enough not to have dentures I had to use the little flat round tin scripted "Steradent" containing foul tasting pink tooth powder[no toothpaste in those days] which probably was of very little use,as our visits to the school dentist at Spring Garden Lane proved.

++

   When I wanted to do something different I would always turn to the trusty pale blue Raleigh bicycle complete with its Sturmey Archer gears,attached to the handlebars next to the white rubber hand grips.Just behind the saddle was a small leather case carrying a spanner and a puncture outfit in its small white tin marked "Dunlop".The tin contained a tube of glue,rubber patches,crayon,chalk ,and sandpaper,enough to repair a hole in the inner tube of the tyre.Front and back lights were powered by a small dynamo, which was powered by me,my pedalling turning the wheels to produce a useable but weak light.The last accoutrements,apart from the bell were a red reflector on the rear mudguard and a white hand pump fixed to the cross bar.
  Adequately prepared with a drink and sandwiches in a brown ex-army rucksack strapped on our back we would be off...where? Well most times it was an adventure which ended wherever we found ourselves and that could be fifteen minutes down the road or two hours away down many winding anonymous roads.
  We would leave Nanas in Leesland Road and when we reached "The Foresters Arms"public house at the junction with Anns Hill Road we had our first predicament, should we go left or right.We would sit discussing the merits of each direction,why we hadn't decided this before I have no idea.Turn left and it would almost certainly be the

short journeys to Privett Park or Stokes Bay...turn right and that would open up greater prospects.

 Right it was,up over Anns Hill Arch, I struggled to pedal up the steep incline,stopping on the top I would be lucky at times to see one of the two steam trains which visited Gosport daily.Whether a stop or not we would then descend the bridge at a breakneck speed to meet the junction with Brockhurst Road where a set of brick built underground toilets adorned the junction.As far as I remember the only time I went in them was when a car in which I was a passenger [A pale blue Triumph Herald] crashed into their entrance when miscalculating the turn from Brockhurst Road.

 This time the junction proved an easier decision to make as to turn right would eventually return you home and we had only just started out.Thus ensuring my bicycle clips were securing the flapping trouser legs,preventing them from getting caught in the chain off we pedalled. Up Brockhurst Road past Molloys,the newsagent on the corner of Cambridge Road,then passing Stapletons,the hardware shop and Roy's,the grocers we headed on towards Brockhurst. Past the end of Military road,before Brune Park School had been even thought of,avoiding the buses which used the triangular junction,complete with another public toilet block in which to take a break,we headed single file for Rowner,Fareham,or back towards Gosport,

 Sometimes the journey would finish here and we would park up our bikes,scramble through the undergrowth and head towards the moat of Fort Brockhurst.At other times we would head out to Hardway or Elson,or onwards to Rowner where the road at that time was little more than a country lane leading over the railway line by way of a single track brick

walled bridge,no footpath then so you took your chance if walking,for the longer rides to Fareham.Lee on the Solent or beyond.

 I can remember the slow unhurried rides,no pressures,time to think,time to see what was around me,time to learn and all of it leaving me with the memories that remain today.

++

 The war had ended over ten years previously and the National Health Service,inaugurated by Aneurin Bevan in 1947 was coming up to celebrate its first decade.Doctors surgeries tended to occupy large Edwardian and Victorian two and three storey houses,the ground floor being the surgery,the upper floors being their home.It was like this at my doctors,Dr Raperports in Stoke Road.He was a tall thin immaculately dressed gentleman and his surgery was as immaculate as the man himself.From the uneven pavement outside you walked up a bridge of well scrubbed steps with handrails of black iron railings, which also surrounded the front of the building,thus preventing you from falling into the basement yard below.The heavy black door with its well polished brassware had at the side the accompaniment of a polished brass plaque extolling the name of the medical incumbent.Dr Raperport,complete with his medical qualifications for all to see.
 Pushing the door open you entered a high ceilinged hallway from which led several doors.you entered one into a room with chairs around the edge and a hatch in one wall.A knock on the hatch and it was opened by a lady who identified our name and invited us to take a seat.When it was your turn the announcement led you to another door which led to the surgery where the doctor was sitting.On entering it was almost like an inner sanctum where the doctor was treated with a certain reverence and you only spoke when he addressed you.All of the rooms had one thing in common...they were painted green!!
 Having completed your consultation you would wait in the waiting room until the hatch in the wall opened and you were called to collect any potion which had been prescribed.
 If the relevant item was unavailable you collected a handwritten prescription and headed down the High Street to Boots the chemists.The dispensing area was adorned with large glass

flagons full of colourful liquids and labelled in black script or copperplate inscribed latin inscriptions.There was also a large wooden chest with a myriad of slim brass handled drawers containing various powders,potions and pills.
 Suitably supplied one would wend their way home with correctly packaged and labelled cure-alls...but very rarely antibiotics.

+++

 Back in the 1950's and early 1960's things were natural,as nature intended then progress and technology arrived and everything started to become almost artificial and false.A walk down a street once lined with lime trees had become barren,no more providing any shelter for bees,the trees "pollarded" or more correctly butchered by an inept tree surgeon.No more the beetles with their magnificent horns,wander the pavements forlornly searching for a mate.Farther along as you enter the lane.dusk is falling here just the same as every year before,but

No more the may bugs or even the bats
Just silent scurries disturbing some rats
On to the cornfields now turning golden
No patches of colour like poppies of olden

No plant life at all that would have been there
We are totally consumed no room to spare
The ditches and hedgerows that bordered the fields
Seem gone forever the price of good yields

The shelter provided has gone away too
No wonder that now we hear not the cuckoo
The flocks of farm birds the buntings and finches
We see them no more from distant flight flinches

No shelter no food and so little cover
There weakness exposed by our lack of bother
The beaches we walked on were covered in holly
We longer linger in thought with our brolly

No more the plover at nest on the shingle
The shoreline now strewn with.......
We now have a last chance to put matters right
To correct all our wrongs and put back our delights.

In order to do this we have to start now
Tomorrow's too late and may already be
But we must start to try and leave some legacy
All of the chemicals we use everyday

The plastics the rubbish that we throw away
If we wish to continue the way that we act
We must be prepared to face up to the fact;
We will have no future to live for.

++

  A few weeks had passed since the trout tickling experience up in the Meon valley and I had been convinced,in spite of my enthusiasm that the same process would not be practical on Stokes Bay beach.....one thing there were no trout and secondly sea water splashing into our eyes as the waves rolled made it impossible to see!
  However constant pestering by myself did have [what to Me]were its just deserts.Deserts which a while later proved to be more than I could eat!!
  Thus it was that on a half term break in May we had exhausted the Maypole rituals and found Nana taking me on my first fishing

expedition.We travelled by bus to North Cross Street and entered Murphys much vaunted emporium where it was fabled you could buy anything.Where a young boy wouldn't be disappointed by the array of rods,reels ,hooks.like you wouldn't see anywhere else,but most importantly they sold the holy grail,ragworm for bait could be purchased there.I don't know how much money changed hands but to Nana it must have been an immense amount.Excitedly I ran down North Street past Arnett's the fishmongers,across the High Street passing Hoopers, the other fishmongers on the corner and down South Street.We were on our way and I was convinced that the fish I was about to catch would be far larger than any of those adorning the marble slabs.On down towards the creek,across the green surrounding the church our destination came in view..Pneumonia Bridge,I ran excitedly forward and up the bridge accompanied by shouts of "go careful ".and eventually a weary Nana laden like a working packhorse caught up.No time to be lost and the fishing tackle was set up and baited...with similarly bated breath the line was cast out and there lay a problem.....due to the low tide even using all the line the poor wriggling worm only managed to get about twelve inches,or a foot above the water level and I swear to this day the fish were coming to the surface with tears of laughter in their eyes knowing they were out of reach of the lure.

 Frustrated.disappointed and with more than a few tears we weaved the path back to Leesland Road even stopping for a picnic in Walpole Park but it did little to raise my spirits,I tiredly went indoors with Nana saying as we arrived home"there's always another day" and there was..unfortunately with similarly disastrous endings,but we will go there on another day.

++

Yesterday someone sent me a photograph from before the second world war......In 1949 Nurse Skinner lay me on the dressing table in the front bedroom at Oxford Road and cut my tongue...I was tongue-tied and by now many probably wish I had stayed that way!!.....both items are connected but I have no memory of either as I was unaware at that time..

Today we learn of the damage we are causing our wildlife by the actions we have taken in our pursuit of producing more of everything,ever faster to a population which is rapidly increasing and out of control.

Looking back I remember the way we were and regret the things we have lost or are losing We could walk to the countryside,it was not far away now we have to drive,sometimes for miles before we see anything remotely rural.We have lost that proximity as urbanisation sprawls further and further as it encroaches relentlessly into the vanishing countryside..Even the green spaces within the conurbations,be they gardens or parks have become smaller,tree lined streets have all but vanished..

Even when we reach the countryside we crave for, it is vastly different from what we had when I was a child.I could then have walked along verdant river banks, lining crystal clear fast flowing streams in which you could see trout laying motionless on the gravel bottom.Now most water courses are a mere trickle of human effluent and chemical laden water killing off what remains of plants like water crowfoot,marsh marigolds,water mint and brookline speedwell due to our thirst for water extraction,watercress vanished because of the pollution.

The water meadows over at North Boarhunt used to teem with dragonflies,moths,bees and richly coloured butterflies.Acrobatic swallows, house and sand martins, competing with bats for the insect feast would skim the grasses,sedges and vibrant flowers as they scooped up the multitude of insects hovering above the ground..Vivid pink ragged robin,delicate lilac ladies smock and exotic native orchids are now rare.... another victim of water extraction.

The hazel coppice near Worlds End no longer homes the bodger,who, laboriously working his foot powered lathe would make the chair legs for the furniture maker,nor the sound of his colleague who used to cut the peasticks,make besom brooms, hurdles and produce charcoal from a kiln he had deeper in the woods,the only clue being a wisp of wood smoke drifting through the tree canopy.

Small neat fields all gated [with five bar gates] and surrounded by hawthorn hedges,ploughed by a brace of horses,or grazed by a herd of lazy cows are all gone.The flocks of yellowhammers buntings,finches,linnets and warblers that made the hedgerows alive have all but vanished.The fields which gave them food by lying fallow overwinter and had a different crop every year are now sown almost immediately after harvest,even crop rotation seems to have outlived its usefulness.

In amongst the whiskered barley,wheat,rye and quaking oats grew red poppies,pink corncockles,white daisies and yellow and purple heartsease but these have gone too killed by weed killers and pesticides Partridges,pheasants and corncrakes would hurry about busily between the varieties of cereals hungrily picking at grubs and fallen seeds.

Cuckoos are now rarely heard no longer the harbingers of summer,with them the song of the rising skylark,the nightingales melody and the tik-tik of the tiny wren.

Oh and the photo?...for the first time I saw a picture of my mum and it was worth the wait of nigh on threescore and ten years!
++

Wednesday was a particularly good day when we were on summer holidays from school.After dinner on a Wednesday having consumed the usual meal of stew and dumplings,usually followed by bread and butter pudding I would get ready to go on my travels whilst Nana washed up..

The same journey was undertaken every week,although the route varied occasionally depending on whether the incoming tide had encroached on the road alongside Alver Creek.

We would start off going down Leesland Road,cut through Tribe Road and then down to Whitworth Road,entering into Gordon Road.At this point we would either go down Foster Road and rest in Foster Gardens where I would sit on the low wall of the circular fishpond, full of goldfish which would come to the surface when I trailed my hand in the lukewarm water,dressed resplendent in waxy yellow and pink water lily blooms in summertime .Alternatively we would go down Green Lane looking out for stag beetles which were numerous at that time.The black males were resplendent with their large antlers and sometimes could be seen engaged in battle with an adversary or pursuing a smaller brown female..fascinating to a seven year old.

If we took the Foster Garden route we would head on past the bowling club and then follow the stony path of the old railway line towards Clayhall.In summer it was painted in the colours of yellow trefoil,purple vetch or the pink and white candy stripe trumpets of a small bindweed.When we reached the end at Clayhall Road the creek,we had walked beside petered out into mudflats and beds of sea lavender and thrift, as we left the old railway and made our way to The Haven where my uncle and aunt lived.

The route from the end of Green Lane led past Alverstoke School, down past St. Mary's Church and if the creek road was flooded,cutting of our route to the old railway line, we would have to continue walking, turning at the children's home down Clayhall Road.Walking briskly past Broderick Hall and the brick tower we came to a small field,bramble bushes around its edges,an old bath filled with water stood in a corner betraying the fact it always contained a pony or two.From here it was only a short distance further crossing the old disused Stokes Bay railway line,passing the creek and then left into the The Haven,a little grocers on the opposite of the road as you entered.

Why was it a good day.....well Aunt and Uncle had a black and white television and as we arrived at a quarter to two I could watch "Bill and Ben and Little Weed".For some time I thought that this was the only children's programme,it was indeed the only one that I ever saw for a long time.Eventually when Dad bought a television I found out that they were on everyday except the weekends.......Monday storybook.....Tuesday Andy Pandy,Teddy and Looby-Lou....Thursday Rag Tag and Bobtail and Friday The Wooden Tops along with Sam,the farmhand,Jenny,Willy,the children and naughty Spotty dog!!

Simple but effective children's entertainment but to us it was the most fascinating television....but then we didn't have technology.....which was probably not a bad thing.

++

Maybe it was because of necessity,maybe because the way people reacted after the war but everything when I was growing up was surrounded by a routine.It didn't matter what was done it was always the same pattern,the same day,the same meal, if something changed there must be something wrong.The meals were predictable daily,the daily chores were the same and you could tell the time and day by the routines that were unswervingly followed.

Dinner as the midday meal was called,not lunch,was always at twelve o'clock.Tea-time was always at four o'clock.You didn't ask what time meals would be ready as you already knew,the same time everyday and woe betide if you were late.

You knew the previous week.month,even year what you would have on your plate...Sunday roast..Monday cold meat and bubble and squeak...Tuesday shepherds pie....Wednesday Stew with dumplings "to fill you up",Thursday liver and bacon....Friday fish and chips...Saturday sausages...nothing ever changed.

All shops closed at midday,dinner was the big meal of the day and every Wednesday and Saturday afternoon very few shops

opened,Saturday afternoon was the time for football or cricket.They opened at the same time and closed at the same time.You could tell the time from when the milkman and postman delivered,the daily routine was the same for even the delivery people..Monday..washday, the dapper moustached Mr Chase would collect the rent [I recall numerous occasions being told to behave as Mr Chase would be here at ten o'clock]...Tuesday ironing and the grocery delivery from the Co-op...Wednesday Nana would go and visit my uncle in Alverstoke...Thursday she drew her pension at Whitworth Road post office,followed by a trip down to Gosport High Street....Friday was baking and bathing day....Saturday saw us collecting the meat for the weekend, followed by football in the afternoon and then the day of rest....Sunday with visits to the cemetery and church.
 The only change to this would be if there was an unexpected disaster...someone had died or a national calamity!
 Monday to Friday Grandad would come up Leesland Road at a quarter to twelve having been in The Junction for his pint of bitter returning home from work ,a little part time cleaning job at Burtons the tailors in the High Street,on the corner of Bemisters Lane.
 Mr Shepard,who walked with a slight limp would arrive with fruit and vegetables delivered by horse and cart, as would Mr Stanley the coal and log man the same times and days every week.Even the gas meter collector would be totally predictable These things weren't as mundane as one may surmise as the predictability enabled you to plan with some certainty the fitting in of less important everyday tasks.Not waiting in all day for deliveries....not having clean clothes.....rarely running out of supplies....stretching out food with certainty...having enough food for visitors....and having enough to pay the bill when it was due...things I'm afraid very much in the past.
 Patience,thrift,planning,common sense......what more did you need!

+++

Welcome to no 80.... I am sure they won't mind you visiting.We are stood outside a brick terrace house with a slate roof and white painted sash windows.The way in is through a heavy brown painted door resplendently decorated with polished brass knocker,letterbox and door knob having crossed a scrubbed stone doorstep,a brass plate protecting the wooden door cill.

Entering the passageway which ran along the right side of the house we walk on a linoleum covered floor, with high cream painted skirting boards,above which a brown shiny paper rose to the waist high dado rail.Above that a creamy paper rose up to meet a distempered ceiling,the walls only broken by the doorway and staircase on the left side The doorway on the left was just as you had entered and led to the "front room" which was only used for special events like the lying of the coffin,overnight, before a funeral.It had a black simple fireplace with a black ebonised overmantle and large mirror above.Two simple white vases decorated with violets stood either end of the mantlepiece and the only lighting was from a single gaslight.There was a sofa and two chairs,a small wooden table in front of the window and a woollen rug on the floor.On the narrow cream painted window ledge was the front door key which could be accessed by opening the ever unfastened sash window in case I came home before the other residents!.Good idea when people could be trusted but the lock in the door was too high for me to reach so it was not an option for me.

At the opposite end of the narrow hallway on the left was the staircase up to the two double bedrooms, a dark coloured carpet runner held in place with heavy brass carpet rods to protect the wooden treads.

Reaching the top the smallest of landings separated two identical bedrooms,one at the back,one at the front.Both had small tiled fireplaces above which there was a narrow shelf to put the enamel candlesticks on when you came to bed.There were enormous double beds made of green cast iron frames with architectural bed ends topped with brass in each room,these were dressed with crisp ironed white cotton sheets and a large bolster under the duck feather pillows supported my head when sleeping.

 Returning down stairs we entered the living room sparsely decorated and furnished but functional.The dark wooden sideboard,with two drawers with doors under stood on the right of the room holding a few simple ornaments and a chiming wooden clock,wound up by a large key everyday without fail.The mantle shelf on the opposite side of the room had a couple of decorative chinese vases and two black elephant figures.Under this shelf was the only source of heating,a coal fire with cardinal red hearth and small brass fender.To the left was a double cupboard,the top containing groceries and a smaller cupboard beneath which had a wooden cutlery tray,tablecloth and the condiment set.Next in the corner was the meter cupboard,a full size door behind which stood a large brown tin blanket box and the gas meter,this was where we hid in the thunderstorms.To the right of the fire stood a waist high bamboo cane table on top of which stood a brown bakelite radio attached to a glass acid battery on the shelf beneath.Mains electricity hadn't arrived at number eighty as Nana didn't want it,she preferred gas.

 The lighting was provided from a single gas light hanging from the centre of the ceiling.Making up the furniture was a wooden table and four chairs,an old adjustable armchair for the man of the house, another armchair opposite it for the lady and a settee covered in a brown oilcloth fabric.Finishing the decor hung a picture of three children and a picture of the battleship HMS Indefatigable, finally one of the Queen as a mark of loyalty and homage.

 Entered from this room was the scullery furnished with a wooden storage cupboard.an upright larder,scrubbed,bleached wooden table,a copper boiler,freestanding gas cooker and Belfast sink.All stood on a clean stone floor worn from constant scrubbing.The loo of course was outside and the "bathroom" hung from the scullery wall above the copper.

Where are we I hear you ask....the year is 1957....no eighty is in Leesland Road.....and I am there with my Nana and Grandad.

++

 I sit surrounded by a cacophony,a wall of impenetrable constant noise and I think back to the days when I was growing up.In those times after the tumultuous incessant bombardment of wartime Britain you could " hear a penny drop " now it would need to be a "fifty pence piece"Yes there were mechanised sounds,the sounds of cars,propeller driven planes the hissing and whistling of steam trains but these were fairly unobtrusive and appeared occasionally,in the background not incessant as now.
There was "the sound of silence" and we knew where to seek it out and enjoy it.....the sound of what should have been there and not what had replaced it!
 I could walk or ride to places and hear.......well what could I hear.In Ann's Hill Cemetery were gravestones, in the old part surrounded by long grass and ox-eye daisies,where bees buzzed and crickets chirruped.The breeze could be heard whispering through the leaves and the tall trunks of the cypress trees would emanate the odd creak as the wind became stronger and the branches rose and fell.
I could hear the thunder rolling in off the sea at Stokes Bay and the lapping of the sea on the beach or the crashing of the waves against the Haslar sea wall.
 As I walked past the now long gone hedgerows, bordering the fields, at nesting time you could hear the young chicks in the nests clamouring to be fed.In the undergrowth you could hear the rustling of mice,shrews and voles or the louder sound of rabbits scurrying off to hide from a marauding weasel..
 Walking to Gilkicker Point I would be serenaded by high flying

skylarks,the "little bit of bread and no cheese" of the yellow hammer backed up by the melancholy notes of a curlew or the more recognisable sound of the cuckoo on his summer holidays.

Out on the track to Apple Dumpling Bridge as I walked along the grassy stream bank I could hear the plop as water voles entered the water and the guttural calls of frogs or the more distinct sound of a toad in the sandy heath.Warblers,stonechat and buntings chattered excitedly as their little flocks busied themselves around in the yellow prickly gorse and the sounds of flying swans filled the air as they moved their graceful wings,propelling them to an inland roost for the night.

How evocative was that sound of silence compared with now when everything is blocked by that tireless hum,that noise of progress...nothing is truer than the words...Silence is golden.!!

+++

During the school holidays we were for the most times expected to amuse ourselves.On the dreaded "wet days" it was a fairly lonely existence as you peered through the window at the grey wet scene,raindrops running down the panes,longing for it to dry up and be able to get outside.No computers,no television,except for a few hours a day,then only if you were wealthy enough to own one and everyone busying themselves in household chores,too busy to spare any time.

On occasions I had "painting by numbers" sets,usually left over from Christmas but the novelty of those soon wore off as an unsteady hand trespassed into the next segment or I even painted a number with the wrong colour altogether.Newspaper lined the table to prevent spillage on to the surface but still I managed a blob here or there that as if by magic appeared when I began clearing away.

The other alternatives apart from the diecast matchbox cars made by Lesney or the larger Dinky or Corgi models were the construction sets.Meccano was the leader with its metal bars and plates held together with nuts bolts and screws and from which you could build trains and cars.One item I recall was what was the forerunner of Lego,it was made of the most foul smelling brown rubber,guaranteed to give you a headache.The smell of the pop together bricks lingered on your hands and almost invariably the pungent odour made me ill.

Papier mache was another simple pastime making items by covering moulds made from bowls,plates, or anything else that you could build up layer upon layer of old newspaper on,held together with paste made from flour and water.Dried in front of the coal fire, then painted in bright poster paints before invariably in a matter of days discarding them into the fire or dustbin.

The one thing these pastimes had in common was that the majority of these were inexpensive apart from the bought items you had been given for Christmas or Birthdays they were mostly made from recycled 'rubbish" as the one thing there was a shortage of during these times...was spare money.

When you went shopping you didn't ask if you could have a toy that you saw,or expect to return with a 'present' from the shops,bought to keep you quiet,rewards weren't needed, you knew what was expected acceptable behaviour.You didn't have sweets except as a treat and if you had a biscuit outside of mealtimes it was seen as a 'treat' also,eating between meals was frowned upon..We largely amused ourselves,got on and made our own entertainment and however little we had we "were mostly happy with our lot".I remember that even when your birthday or Christmas present was given to you it was a surprise and you didn't always get what you wished for!! If you did it was more by luck than judgement as you were rarely asked what you wanted.....it is largely our generation that decided "ask them to do a list as we may as well give them something they want!!"

I remember vividly when I was seven and was hoping for a shiny red train I had seen in Woolworths,my disappointment at getting a boxed powder blue prayer book was tangible.At the time not what I wanted but I still have that prayer book in its box complete with its inscription from Nana....would I have still had the red toy train?....I doubt it.

++

Looking back this afternoon I realised that when I was growing up just how different life was.It was definitely slower and people possessed so many skills which are now lost to automation,Necessity dictated people's ability to perform tasks manually as they had no other way to do them and people were proud of those skills.
  These were the days of National Service where trades were taught and when you returned to "civvy street" you had been provided with the basis for a lifelong skill with which you could make a living.
  The goods we used were natural,mostly.and we used what was available locally as much as possible.The clothes we wore were cotton,wool,linen even fur as man made fibres were in their infancy,Harris tweed was a heavy luxury woollen cloth and nearly all our shoes were still made from leather .I remember going to school with highly polished shoes and coming home to a cuff around the ear for scuffing them playing football. Short trousers[long ones didn't seem to be worn till teenage years] were made of cotton flannel,undergarments of cotton and woollen hand knitted jumpers,either long or short sleeved completed the uniform.Raincoats were made of gabardine and nearly everybody wore a hat of some kind.The working man wore a flat cap and then as the classes went up you saw trilbys and bowlers.Fishmongers wore straw boaters,often with a blue ribbon around them,fishermen wore sou'westers and the less salubrious individuals wore"pork-pies"!.Factory workers wore overalls,grocers wore brown or white coats and any professional

people,solicitors,doctors and bank managers would always wear suits,normally complete with waistcoats,and carry a briefcase.Butchers and fishmongers would were red and white or blue and white aprons respectfully.In fact uniforms were commonplace in many places where you could identify tradespeople just from their clothes.

 Most people then were comfortable with what was around them but looking back now surrounded by technology and gadgets I wonder how I managed to fill all my time but I can't ever remember being bored.More to the point I felt that having made an item from nothing I had achieved something....sadly I don't feel the same being so automated and pressing buttons!

++

 Easter was over,the time had arrived as the weather improved and the evenings became lighter, to venture out in the car for picnics at the weekend.These would normally take us on a journey north of Fareham up the A32 and then in a variety of directions.One day it would be straight across at the crossroads at Wickham Church,the road running alongside a small stream with adjacent reed beds and quite often you would see the azure blue and orange plumage of a vigilant kingfisher sat on a protruding branch on his fishing duties.We will return to fishing again a little later.

 Carrying on we would travel toward Alton,sometimes heading up past the watercress beds and up onto Old Winchester Hill where we would play ball or I would fly a colourful kite amidst chalk grassy slopes painted with purple vetches,blue scabious and luxuriant and elegant orchids in pinks, purples and browns.

 One day in May 1960 we continued from there down a narrow country lane passing HMS Mercury eventually arriving at the Rising Sun in the village of Clanfield.Our destination was to view the hostelry which Dad had been involved in building,a normal public house but a little special. At the time, as a site agent, Dad was in charge of the most famous pub in the world, according to Reuters news agency. Its claim to fame was that it had been built and readied for business in just twelve hours!!

Other times we would pass Old Winchester Hill continuing to head on through the Meon Valley past the Meon Hut and the Pig and Whistle inns, before heading towards Privett or Alresford Down to enjoy our refreshments. Well enjoy may be a little inaccurate as descriptions go. Soggy tomato and cheese sandwiches, tea which had stewed in a flask, complete with milk, followed by warm victoria sponge, with jam a little rancid, didn't strike me as being the height of luxury.

On the return journey if it was not too late, we would venture off the main road in order to traverse the shallow ford at Exton before rejoining to the normal route. As we travelled down the Meon valley we would detour through the villages of East Meon and Meonstoke, stopping to gaze in the crystal clear, gravel bottomed river to see the brown trout nestling on the riverbed.

It was here that we must return to fishing and where I thought it would be fun to try the human version, angling, as it seemed so exciting.!! Over at Apple Dumpling bridge on Browndown I had managed very well with a net and jam jar, although less successful with the stick, line and bent pin, but the kingfisher had kindled a latent desire by its actions!

What fuelled my interest even more was what I saw next....on the bank of the river was what then we would have called"a country yokei',..an elderly gent in breeches and waistcoat, and as we later found out a Hampshire accent to match his eccentricity, He was lying on his belly on the banks edge with both hands in front of him in the water.

He lay almost motionless and after a short while. with a deft flick of the hands a shining brown trout appeared on the bank next to him!! I watched in awe as the shiny wet fish wriggled on the grass and my eyes opened even wider when the man uttered something quite unintelligible.

It was the first and only time I saw anyone tickle a trout and it never occurred to me that the same way of fishing wouldn't be so effective on Stokes Bay beach.Several months later my bubble was burst.....but that is a memory for the future!

++

  The one subject nobody seemed to talk about in the 1950's was the second world war which had ended in 1945.All around us,everywhere we looked there were signs of the after effects which had as yet not been rectified.There was the bombsite in Leesland road just down from Norman Road where at no 46 Mrs Brown and her baby daughter,Vera had died during a raid from the Luftwaffe in 1941.It had quickly become overgrown with ragwort,veronica and brambles and just a few traces of rubble from the building remained. There was Trinity Church in Gosport High Street,in the cemeteries there were rows of headstones marking the final resting place of both Allied and German military personnel.No malice was shown to the adversary, just sympathy for the loss of such young lives.I remember my Nana in Ann's Hill Cemetery standing,looking and reading with a tear in her eye the name of a teenage German soldier who had lost his life before it had really begun,just nineteen and gone forever....anger,yes,..but no hatred.Elsewhere at Stokes Bay there lay the remnants of unused, damaged concrete pontoons and on Grange Airfield a little fenced compound was littered with parts of war damaged aircraft,awaiting scrap.

  There were gaps,buildings missing,in several roads and the odd military vehicle rumbled its way around from Clarence Barracks but nobody spoke about the events.The exception I remember was on two occasions,apart from Grandad's sojourn in the fruit tree during the aforesaid 1941 raid, and one of those was from the first war.

Grandad was on HMS Indefatigable in the Dardanelles when a Turkish shell went through the deck and joined him in the galley where he was cooking.That brass shell head had stood on the sideboard at Nanas,and now is in the fireplace of my cottage, however the piece of Gibraltar Rock which had stood beside it on Nana's sideboard,[the relevance of which I never found out, vanished when Nana died.

The only time the second world war came up in conversation was one day when Dad had taken us for a ride and picnic up to the Trundle at Goodwood, and on the way back we made a detour through Tangmere.As we passed through the village he told us how he was working for John Hunts the Gosport builders during the war,as he was a builder and suffered with bronchitis his was in a reserved occupation.They were involved in work for the War Department.The following day the Luftwaffe bombed the airfield and left it only partially operational.

Unknown to me when I moved into my cottage on that same day a German escort fighter had during that operation fired at and hit the cottage and a little lad playing in the garden had lost his life.

Stories of sadness but even so the need to be told before they are forgotten.Much happened during the war and after but so much of it has died with the people's memories that held them.

My thoughts are simple,my memories everyday.....but think what those before us could have told and how we maybe should have asked or listened before it became too late.The previous generation to us were very private....kept thoughts to themselves and suffered in that silence.

++

People say that the memories we share show our childhood through rose tinted glasses but needless to say there were times when the memories were painful.It's simply that it is better to remember the good times and just acknowledge that those dark times did exist.This time,however,the memory is one that would change the whole of my life.

It is in fact almost certainly my first clear memory when I was almost five,although there were simpler memories of everyday events which I recall..October 1954...and a bright day with a great adventure ahead.Dad owned a black Ford Prefect but today we had been lent a silver Triumph Renown,quite a luxury car at the time, and big enough for us all,as my aunt and uncle were joining us,to fit into,as it was to be a long journey.The roads were all single carriageway,so the trip would be necessarily slow and thehamper in the boot meant there would be several stops on the way for refreshment and the bathroom.The first of these stops was at Hindhead outside a large hostelry which had from memory the name of Angry or Hungry[or possibly Happy] Cheese and was the stopping place for charabancs on route to the seaside from London.

Suitably refreshed and after a few more miles there were more stops,each requiring a cup of tea from the flask and each followed by one of numerous car spotting and I-spy games to pass the time and alleviate the boredom,eventually we arrived at our destination...St. Albans in Hertfordshire.We pulled up outside a large austere barrack like building with a neatly manicured green lawn around it, enclosed with a black iron railing.

There at last the adults got out of the car,walked through an impressive archway and entered the building, apart from my aunt who waited with my sister and me outside.After a short space of time,Dad appeared at a ground floor window with my Nana,Grandad and Aunt and Uncle.Along with the group was the reason for the journey and subsequent visit,my Mum.She waved at us and we waved back,we hadn't seen her for a week but even now we couldn't go in to give her a hug, as in those days children were not allowed in hospital wards,and recovery from her operation was a long way off .A final wave,a few tears and the adults came out chatting and smiling anticipating the long

journey back to Gosport,discussing the next steps in Mum's treatment and when she was likely to be allowed home.
  The return journey was uneventful and us children although happy and excited slept for most of it as we were exhausted,we even missed the refreshment stops.
  We had seen Mum for the first time since she was taken from the bed she had rarely moved from in four years into a white ambulance to Guys Hospital in London, where the eminent surgeon Mr Ross had performed a pioneering heart operation and sent her to St Albans Hospital to recuperate.For the first time we looked forward to Mum returning home being able to play with us like normal children.
  We arrived home at Oxford Road in the dark and with street lamps which were not very effective we hardly spotted the figure in the shadows ....as we sleepily were taken indoors we became aware of the figure at the front door who was engaged in a conversation with Dad.Dad was becoming agitated,upset,as the conversation progressed,and as the policeman left the atmosphere became one of sadness and we were hurried to bed with the news that Mum had died.She had passed away soon after we left the hospital...our dreams were shattered as was our immediate future.

++

  How so much has changed since time I was a kid.It's not till you look at what is seen as normal now that we realise just how much technology rules our lives similar to the industrial revolution.Everything is geared to doing things faster and easier but nobody has any time to do anything so is the effort actually beneficial or"a waste of time"There are many things which have enhanced our lives but undoubtedly in doing so not actually made them any better,
  As the"labour saving devices" became more common,more people wanted them so paid them on "hire purchase"and to pay for this credit

the women who had stayed at home started to need to work and the recognised family unit slowly, disappeared,Ready meals were produced to combat the gap which appeared in the family kitchen,balanced meals were no longer prepared by"mum" and obesity and worry about calories started to develop..

We are all now looking at the effect the present society is having on the future and looking back but it is really a product of what happened during the 1950's that started it all.

I loved growing up in the 1950's and can see why, when we were able to take time and wait, instead of the endless impatience and need to do things yesterday which now prevails on us all.

Good weather,sunshine,summer just around the corner and the time was right for picnics.The picnic was almost an institution,it was an opportunity to get out into the fresh air,an opportunity to spend time with family and relax,it was the highlight of the weekend.By the time I was a teenager the picnic was developing into the barbeque,the one big difference being that it was performed at home more than in the countryside.

The biggest picnic we had of course was the Queen's Coronation when it took the form of a street party.Leesland Road had Union Jack bunting hanging from window to window across the road,the road closed so we could celebrate safely.Everyone brought out their dining chairs and to make enough seats wooden planks were placed across two chairs to form a bench.

The tables groaned with simple food but plenty of it.Jam, paste,Heinz sandwich spread.A Variety of home made cakes and buns and huge bowls of trifle accompanied by tinned IXL brand peaches,pears and mandarin segments in syrup.Not be missed were the colourful jellies,strawberry,lemon,lime or raspberry and strawberry and chocolate blancmanges in various shapes of rabbits,castles or just simple mounds from a pudding basin.Each child,including myself, was given a memento of the al-fresco banquet,in my case a card,cup plate and saucer others a commemorative coin.The celebration continued well

into the evening when the food changed to cold meat,pickles,crusty bread and alcoholic beverages,rather than lemonade or "pop",
as the mums and dads,grans,grandads and aunts and uncles took their turn.Hundreds of neighbours shoulder to shoulder laughing and enjoying themselves and being,well,neighbourly with everyone knowing everyone else,any disagreements being forgotten in the euphoria of the splendid occasion.

++

After the occasion of the grand Coronation day "picnic" everyone seemed to be more oriented to eating outside and bank holidays would see huge numbers of people heading to favourite places if the weather was favourable.Baskets were filled with the usual cutlery and crockery and either distributed between willing carriers or into a car
boot depending how far you were heading.The bowls of fresh salad,lettuce,tomato,cucumber and spring onion from the allotment, were covered in clean damp tea towels to keep them fresh and little packs of sandwiches were folded in greaseproof paper.A pork pie, may be the treat of the day was carefully cut into wedge shaped slices when we arrived at the picnic site for the great anticipated event.Tea would be carried in Thermos flasks and home made lemonade in similar containers.The tea from the flasks had at time a musty taste but we didn't mind.
 The travelling rugs were laid on the ground and whilst the ladies spread out the tea on the table,the same place as the chairs...the
 ground,the children and menfolk would wander off into the woods or fields to explore the area and educate the kids in flora and fauna.Insects would be captured and then released,minnows and sticklebacks would be caught and carried home in jamjars,butterflies netted,in the same nets we had fished with, and then let go.

Soon a shout would come, not a moment too soon as we had worked up an appetite, and a stampede took place to get back to the food first and consumed as quickly as possible. Constant chastising of "where are your manners, don't speak with your mouth full and chew your food" came from mums and dads, "what's the hurry. Why was there such a hurry?....well as soon as we had all eaten we would play cricket, rounders or football with all the family taking part before we packed up to return back home. Wearily we would wend our way back home jolly signing accompanying the path back home at the end of a wonderful day out. The cost to us very little now in the twenty first century, the equivalent cost an absolute fortune, as most people would be happier paying huge amounts for less wholesome takeaway food and the convenience of not having to prepare it themselves.

++

Memories are made from out of our past
Some doomed to dim but others will last
Good ones and bad ones they each have a place
Each has a moment to fill in a space

We look back with longing creating the best
Of the time we remember when we couldn't rest
Running and playing every hour of the day
Whether running in fields or picking the may

We smiled and laughed as we played in the streams
And bundled up senses to use in our dreams
Which we then stored as memories which time will not steal
The experience of living be good or be ill

As we grow up with games and many good friends

We wish every day the adventures won't end
Climbing high trees and jumping off walls
Picking up thoughts that the future recalls

That time is now..... as we're in our future
And now is the time that those memories live
In our minds to give pleasure when we can relax
Passing on history and handing it back

To the young generation who are just starting out
Remember the times when times casted no doubt
In forming their memories that they can pass on
And perpetuate the senses until we will be gone.

++

 Easter in 1957 had fallen late in April and by that time the clocks had been forward for a month, the weather had started to get nicely warmer and the time for weekend picnics to the wilds of Hampshire had arrived. Dad,was lucky to have come into some money,having been part of a syndicate who had been fortunate enough to have won the football pools meaning he could afford the luxury of a car.At the time it was a black Ford Prefect,most cars were black, the number of which was BTP 405.It had wire spoked wheels and running boards at the side along with orange semaphore arm signals which came out from the pillars just behind the front doors.Most of the time however the driver used various hand signals out of the window,up and down meant slowing down,straight out meant turn right and a circular motion signalled a turn to the left
The car I recall dated from the late '1940'S and travelled at a speed which today would have been snail like,its capability was slow at best but at times when loaded was even slower.
I can recall occasions when the men alighted and pushed the car with

women and children still inside,especially if it was raining and the incline became too much.No seat belts,a gear shift which was itself difficult to use,double de-clutch was the normal, and a vicious starting handle to crank it with if the battery was a bit flat or lifeless.

I remember the day we headed over the back roads of Portsdown Hill through North Boarhunt where we followed the lanes flanked by sandy banks showing signs of fox activity, passing The Horse and Jockey pub we continued along the narrower lanes till we arrived where there was a large dairy farm on the corner.The herd of black and white cattle stood passively waiting to be milked and the typical farmyard smell of silage and manure filled the air.As we turned up this lane we entered an area of hazel copse which was just starting to come into life with catkins,lambs tails as we knew them, hanging from the trees,a carpet of yellow primroses,purple dog violets,and white wood anemones poking in profusion through the leaf litter on the ground.Half way up this lane we pulled up to pick a bunch of these spring flowers,an action not frowned on in those times and suddenly my uncle spotted a large "birds nest" in an adjacent holly tree.It was never going to be an easy tree to climb but to see what eggs were in it clouded all logic,so the hazardous ascent began.

After great difficulty the nest was reached and I am afraid that at that point the problem became evident.Gingerly putting his hand in to get the egg,it came out far faster, there was emitted a loud yelp and the ground was reached at a speed faster than the car was capable of doing………the owner of the nest was not amused in having its home invaded.To the grey squirrel, his drey was his castle and he rightly repelled all invaders.

Nursing his wounds my uncle sat on a tartan woollen travelling blanket laid on a grassy bank in the now tranquil and silent countryside whilst the rest of us began eating our paste,corned [bully]beef or spam sandwiches or sometimes just jam sandwiches.,washed down with tea from a silver flask and the only luxury not the food but the occasion itself.

Evenings had begun to get lighter so then the more time I could spend outdoors.enjoying the fresh air.Most times it would a trip up to Privet Park in order to play football with my pals.The normal goalposts were taken down by the council groundsman after the weekend matches so we had to make do with piles of coats spaced out by pacing out the distance between"posts" not always accurately I must say If you were the "goalie" then you would slyly reduce the goal width if you thought it was too wide or you weren't a reliable goalkeeper.it wasn't exactly cheating just a form of gamesmanship.

There would be cries of "on me 'ead" when a corner was taken,hoping that the kicker couldn't kick it that high as if it did reach your head the weight of the leather laced ball[even worse if wet] would send you home with a headache and at least six inches shorter.

Most of us played football in leather boots with proper laces and leather studs which were nailed onto the boot and often the nails worked through the sole.You would arrive home and the shoe last would come out ,the boot placed on it and the nails flattened,a simple solution to a major problem.

Some summer evenings we would have a cricket match with a wicket made of a bag or pile of clothes,the length of the pitch having very little relation to a real one,the ball a well worn red one cadged from a cricket club,or more often a tennis ball,no pads and an old bat which was almost as tall as some of the batsmen.

If there was no ball and tennis ball was used the game tended to be a shorter event as there was always a good batsmen who would hit the ball for miles and soon exhausted all the fielders.

Other evenings we would play tennis wearing plimsolls,given little grip on built up grit which seemed to build up on the tennis courts at Stokes Bay,situated near the end of Jellicoe Avenue next to a little miniature golf site.Suitably tired we would make our way home as dusk fell and if we could club together threepence we would walk up Whitworth Road to the chippy and buy a portion of chips,ask for scraps and liberally laced with salt and vinegar eat them from last week's copy of The Portsmouth Evening News.On wealthier evenings we may have had a treat of a pickled egg.pickled onion or even an orange skinned saveloy accompanied by a buttered roll shared between all of us,often as many as six or seven.

++

 Many afternoons when I was at Nanas in Leesland Road as with most little boys I was witness to an exciting event,a little boy's dream.
It started with a distant whistle and when I heard that I would run out the front door,cross the junction with Norman Road,hoping there were no cars and career down the road to the railway crossing at Lees Lane.If I had timed it right I would arrive at the wire mesh fence at the crossing gates just as the locomotive arrived to wait for the crossing keeper to come down from his signal box.Percy was an elderly man in a peaked cap,almost as old as the railway and he would close the heavy wooden gates by hand.Each gate was topped with red paraffin light when dark and had a giant red warning disc in the middle of the gate.
 The driver and fireman would wave and as the train moved forward a plume of steam,soot and smoke would go high into the sky,even more spectacular a sight when the rails were wet or greasy.The train consisting of goods wagons,oil tankers and the ever present guards van moved off towards Gosport station to offload first at Ashleys[Sandersons] wallpaper factory,the coal yard,outside Gosport Station and nearly always its final destination the victualing depot for the MoD at Clarence Yard.Out of our sight I hurried back up Leesland Road past the bombsite where we sometimes played and then into

Norman Road.Past the "witches" white house,where a really harmless old lady lived,around the corner past Treloars demolition yard,lately T J Hughes, and then run alongside the railings bordering the playground of St.Mary's School before turning right up to Ann's Hill arch.I would then sit on the wall and wait patiently.Suddenly you heard the pulsing of the approaching locomotive which could have been anything....a Q1 "coffee pot",a Bulleid pacific from the West Country,Battle Of Britain or Royal Mail classes or maybe just a nondescript tank or goods engine.[I think it was probably whatever was available at Fareham on the day].As it hove into view we waved frantically and as it approached the engine driver would wave.blow the whistle and then rapidly accelerate,shrouding us with the lovely smell of warm damp steam as it went under the bridge on which we stood.

Accelerating away towards the disused Brockhurst Station,we wistfully watched till it was out of view heading over the Military Road crossing on its way to join the mainline at Fareham,sometimes stopping off at Frater or Bedenham to add a wagon to its load.

It was always goods trains as passenger trains had not run since the early '1950's.However I can recall one pea-green locomotive number 30120,which had been restored and preserved pulling a train of passengers dressed in period costume,complete with wigs,on a special occasion and I viewed from Rowner Road arch.

Adventure over I hurried back home to be greeted by Nan saying"where have you been I've told you not to go off like that!! Oh well I'm still here so nothing too bad happened.

++

Next week is Easter.my Nana said temptingly. with the prospect of eggs.possibly small chocolate ones,the possibility to me,having had very little chocolate was a dream come true.Early in the 1950's chocolate was still on ration,I had tasted very little,but what I had eaten I certainly enjoyed.Even when it came off ration it was still limited in availability as sugar remained rationned for a while longer.

The end of Lent had arrived and the giving up of a favourite item[normally sweets,cake,sugar or like]saw us having done our penance of faith,therefore we could now look forward as Maundy Thursday approached to open the weekend's treats.

 School had ended for two weeks and the sounds of "On a green hill far away" had echoed around school assembly as it did each year,then vanished until brought out the next year.We eagerly waited for the "extras" that would herald Good Friday as that day was a bank holiday and people dressed in their Sunday best to celebrate.The first place we congregated was at the bakers shop in the High Street,the spicy aroma wafting from the shop onto the pavement as we queued to buy our Hot Cross Buns,more spicy,much more tasty than today's' offerings,plain buns baked with ample addition of cinnamon ,nutmeg,mixed spice,mixed peel and fruit.The bakers were allowed to open to sell only these buns on Good Friday morning,the only day they were sold,a tradition that had lasted since 1592,when the first Queen Elizabeth made a decree which still made them an enduring and still popular tradition, Clutching the still warm buns we moved along to Arnett's the fishmongers in North Street to purchase fish for dinner unless you were rich enough to purchase fish and chips from the fryer in Whitworth Road next to the hardware shop owned by Mr and Mrs Clogg.

 At this time public houses like The Junction did not open on Good Friday and the seedy bookmakers with its entrance concealed by an obscured glass door,always shut to hide it from prying young eyes,was also closed affording no refuge for the menfolk.

 Either in the morning or evening there was the obligatory church service along with its model depiction of the crucifixion and normally a model of the tomb of Jesus at Gethsemane.

 Formalities over and after consuming the traditional fried fish for dinner,along with parsley sauce, we walked up Leesland Road ,and turning down Wilmot Lane wandered up to the park to play or watch the football.If energetic enough, a walk out to Browndown might be

ventured, whilst Dad and Grandad travelled to Fratton Park to watch Portsmouth, if they were playing a game at home.
 At the end of a tiring day we would retire to bed with our Hot Chocolate,Horlicks or if you were an "Ovaltiney" a mug of Ovaltine.

++

Easter Saturday was less exciting spent baking and preparing the very important Easter Eggs,the only treat being the chance to lick any remaining cake mix from the mixing bowl.Fresh newly laid eggs were collected from the run at the end of the garden, washed,and dried.I then sat at the newspaper covered table to decorate the shells with colourful poster paints,whilst Nana finished the baking,looking in from time to time to check my progress.These gaudily painted gifts were at this time often the only Easter Eggs we had,boiled and eaten with "soldiers" for Easter Sunday breakfast,by the time they reached the table most of the decoration had washed off.It wasn't till the latter end of the 1950's that small hollow chocolate eggs became more plentiful and popular,a distant product from today's highly decorated and over packaged confections.
 Church on Easter Sunday would provide a little posy of flowers for Nana,the alternative a little bunch of primroses and violets picked from the copse or woods we visited in the afternoon after the pilgrimage to the cemetery and the family graves If it was warm and fine enough we would take a picnic of sandwiches and the traditional marzipan based Simnel cake,in later years replaced by a Tunis cake purchased from the grocers,packed in a red tin.The picnic rounded off by a game of cricket or rounders on a pitch reminiscent of a ploughed field we made our way home,to do a similar exercise on Easter Monday....Easter celebrated till the next year!.

++

When we were young we played in the park
We played in the street until it was dark
We played in the sun and we played in the rain
But even when wet we would rarely complain

When we were young very little was new
Hand me downs from our siblings but they were made do
We knew we were treated as best they were able
But parents always provided good food on the table

When we were young we helped where we could
By tidying up tables or help collect wood
We always said thank you and always said please
Sometimes we would shiver but never would freeze

When we were young we learnt right from wrong
We enjoyed helping others and natural birdsong
The flowers and fauna we had all around
We watched from a distance never making a sound

When we were young all was seemingly carefree
Wading in streams,crossing fields,climbing trees
We would walk through the corn and lay in the hay
We would visit the church and kneel down and pray

When we were young we made do and mend
We reused and recycled with no money to spend
We assisted each other without batting an eye
We experienced the living and pain when they died

Now I am older I reflect and look back
The pathways the alleys the short muddy tracks
The times I enjoyed when I played in the park
Playing unfettered from morning to dark

++

  New adventures began when we moved to Rowner,one of which was to make our way to Lee On The Solent, you could walk it at a brisk pace without virtually seeing anybody.Once you turned down past Lockyers, the butchers shop at the end of the small parade of shops you were in Brune Lane which then had naval married quarters on the left and nothing but green fields on the right.
  A short walk and the lane had a little bridge leading over a little stream surrounded by reed beds which was at times no more than just a trickle.Crossing over you arrived at a poorly defined footpath linking the two areas of the Lee on the Solent golf course.On your right was a little copse, blue with bluebells in May,on the other side was vegetation consisting of yellow prickly gorse,broom of the same colour and young lime green fronds of bracken which formed a dense brown mat in winter,as it died off.
  At this point the road split in two,taking the right fork and you would pass the golf clubhouse and the two old cottages with pink roses growing up them,Here too was the clubhouse shop where I could sell second hand golf balls I had found,sometimes the finding was not an accurate description as it was me picking a ball up and hiding before the golfer arrived.As I walked along the road to join the main road leading to Lee on the Solent the golf course ended and a couple of fields with horses appeared as I rounded the bend,I remember walking this lane one hot summer's day with aunts and uncles and they jumped out of their skins when an adder slithered across the hot tarmac surface.My usual preference was to follow the left fork up Shoot Lane,I

liked this best as it was more leafy and in summer it provided copious amounts of blackberries,the bushes along both sides of the single track thoroughfare.The tempting black juicy fruit were delicious and despite Nana's warning not to eat any till they were washed,"as you might catch polio",her words were largely ignored,as was the risk,although polio at that time still was not totally under control by vaccination. Along the lane as you neared the wonderful old farmhouse at Shoot Farm there stood a wooden table on which rested steel milk churns waiting for collection by the milk lorry,not a tanker,with very little concern for"chill chain regulations"! If you were lucky as well as rabbits you might see stoats or weasels along the way...a weasel"caravan"being a site to savour.Nothing could be more amusing as a family of weasels,nose to tail, crossing from one side of the road to the other in a wiggling procession.

 I walked on past the pigs in the muddy fields,almost devoid of vegetation,passing Cherque Farm,with it's old barn and granary,then as we turned left to take the road to the sea I was able to see the helicopters in HMS Daedalus,in 1959 the innovative hovercraft could be glimpsed when it was being tested.At the time Dad was working for John Hunts as a site agent and was lucky enough to get an early ride in one of the first,the SRN1..

 Wearily I walked past the tennis and rackets club,the days when the rackets were made of wood and catgut and nearly all made by Dunlop or Slazenger, the tennis balls always white.

 Not much further now and Lee on the Solent tower came into view and the promised ice cream and a paddle in the cool sea,the water lapping over my feet on the shoreline helped to soothe the weary body,before I had to point my aching feet back home.

++

 1961,by now I was eleven years old and it was time to leave Leesland school,having taken the eleven plus I was ready to move on to pastures new.This manifested itself in new far horizons and to get there promised to be an adventure in itself.At six thirty in the morning I could be found running for a bus at Rowner crossroads,the bus stop opposite the little twitten that ran behind the garage compound in Masten Crescent..

Once on the bus the conductress in her green uniform and peaked cap issued a ticket from a machine,dispensed after dialling in the fare with a dial similar to an old bakelite phone.Slung around her neck,it hung to the left,hanging on the right side was a leather cash bag hanging off her shoulder waiting to hold the fares she was taking.

The bus rattled along the road,struggling as it climbed Rowner Arch, before arriving at Brockhurst,descending through Elson and down the Crossways,then,now almost full,lurching down Whitworth Road across into Foster Gardens, rejoining Stoke Road at the White Hart and then finally down to Gosport Ferry.

On arrival at the ferry terminal I acquired a ticket from the brick ticket office,then walked down the jetty to the pontoon,in winter a precarious journey due to it being very slippery because of the icy surface.To alight onto the ferry was another trial as the old steam ferries bobbed up and down as I climbed onto the heaving deck and my legs were a little on the short side.Having boarded onto the precarious sloping deck I picked my way around the mass of bicycles and went to where the ship's funnel was,as that was the warmest place to stand,whilst sheltering from the north wind blowing down the harbour,from Portsdown Hill.

I would look to see what submarines were in HMS Dolphin,glance at the numerous warships moored alongside in the Dockyard and as we came to moor at the jetty in Portsmouth the minesweepers became visible in HMS Vernon.The I.O.W ferries would be moored alongside the dock by the railway station,awaiting their cargoes to take across the Solent and two elderly Isle of Wight paddle steamers were moored just off the jetty,a memory of past years.

Having made my way up the slope to the entrance to Portsmouth Harbour Station I concentrated on dodging the sometimes itinerant workers on bicycles hurrying like ants to the dockyard gates,if time, I would peer in the station entrance to see what steam trains might be standing at the platforms..

I then walked up The Hard and passed the trolley buses stood by the dockyard entrance,turning in the opposite direction I passed the cafe and tattoo parlour set in the walls of the railway embankment.Hurrying on I passed the Ladybird clothes factory,under the grey girder railway bridge I lingered for a while, watching the naval guards at the gate of HMS Vernon.Smartly dressed in full uniform,white "blancoed webbing"belt and gaiters contrasting with the navy blue bell bottom trousers,the armed seamen stood at attention.As I turned up towards Cambridge Road I passed on my right the old twin chimneys of the coal fired power station,surrounded by piles of coke the tall chimneys belched out clouds of acrid sulphur laden smoke.Oddly enough,in contrast,on the opposite side of the road was the tree lined grassy expanse of the playing fields of the United Services rugby ground,entered through a stone archway, where in the mid 1960's I watched the famous New Zealand All Blacks play an exciting match against a Royal Navy team..Not too far now as I traversed the small area of waste ground opposite my final destination, and if time allowed I popped into the little sweet shop opposite the gates to the school housed in the old Cambridge Military Barracks..

All this by eight thirty in the morning.I was exhausted from the journey, having lugged a heavy brown leather briefcase,adorned with brass locks,full of heavy books and too much homework,but still I was expected to do a days schooling.We had it so easy then,so I am told,

but surprisingly there weren't many complaints as we didn't have time.It was very much a case of"grin and bear it".

++

 I stood quietly in my garden hankering back to my own childhood. In my garden with my young grandson I was watching blue tits going in and out of the bird box where they appear to already have young.I am lucky living in an old listed building with a very large garden so my grandson can wander around safely.Growing up the small gardens at the back of the terraced house was mostly lacking in all but the commonest of avian creatures,sparrows and pigeons,however I had a far bigger garden,one which the whole country could enjoy.I was transported to my time at that age when my garden was the countryside where I wandered safely through fields or woods and strolled along beaches.In those days nature was to be wondered at,looked for and appreciated,but today although the same things are around we do very little to educate our children to value it.
 Back in the days I would go bird nesting and many young boys collected eggs,not understanding why they were doing wrong,now however many children if they saw a bird's nest they would ignore it!.I would actively search for nests,high and low, to see the subtle differences, understanding not to disturb them,the adage being "look,learn.leave".Sometimes yellow gaping mouths would greet your presence,at other times you wondered at the coloured eggs were yet to conceive.
 I chased butterflies with a cheap net,which on other occasions would double up as fishing net to catch minnows or sticklebacks,in order to see what they looked like,always careful to release them unhurt.I would see what caterpillars they came from and if lucky enough to find a pupa would take it home to see what hatched out from it,careful to note the plant on which I had found it.
 I would pick wildflowers,but not pull them up and would trace leaves and grasses onto sheets of greaseproof paper,alternatively place a flower between sheets of blotting paper,before pressing it under the

weight of several heavy books.I'd compete to find how many different plants I could find,one year finding and identifying over four hundred.I was fascinated by what frogspawn became,first tadpoles and as the legs developed a miniature frog,simple evolution before my own eyes..I searched the grass for slow worms,lizards and newts just to hold them and see what they looked like,careful to avoid the poisonous adder or viper with its chevron pattern.

 I would sit quietly waiting for the wild animals to appear as dusk or dawn approached,squirrels,hares,rabbits,foxes,even the little house mouse next to the fireplace at home but my favourite was the pet worm in my pocket that invoked shrieks of disgust from Nana found as she was doing the washing.

The difference is that children don't do this now and parents don't encourage it,or possibly understand it.If it crawls it gets stamped on,if it flies it gets swatted,if it crosses the road we don't avoid it,we run it over.If we see it injured,we leave it to die,no compassion,no concept of what natural beauty offers.

 During the fifties we saw wildlife as an asset, now in the twenty-first century many times it is just in the way or a nuisance when in fact our actions are destroying the treasures that are so valuable but invisible to children today.

The nineteen fifties growing up in nature was important as much of our time was spent playing surrounded by it.....you don't get that feeling in a sterile room with a screen,it was far more exciting.

++

 Not everyday was full of adventure but most days had something to give us some measure of excitement,something to occupy the time,to alleviate the monotony.It was surprising how little things could give so much pleasure and mean so much.The only difference between then and now was that imagination and effort,was the important ingredients,you made your own entertainment.During the course of a normal week the number of games played in groups,or on your own with just a friend were myriad, British bulldog,kiss chase,hopscotch,statues and numerous uses were invented for using a skipping rope..

The girls would make daisy chains and the boys would play conkers.Toy lorries and cars had imaginary deliveries and adventures on imaginary roads as I played on the pavement at the front of the houses in Leesland Road.

Some of us had soap boxes made from pram wheels,wood and rope enabling us to steer it,or not,as we crashed off the pavement accompanied to squeals of delight,then rolling in the normally deserted road.

The streets were awash with children enjoying their freedom,freedom only curtailed when rain came down or it happened to be Sunday,the religious focus of the week.

Rainy or cold days presented another challenge to rise to but I always found a way of overcoming the problem.Apart from the obvious painting drawing and tracing or the reading of our favourite books,mine was Winnie the Pooh, I made various items,some for me,some for others. Papier mache bowls,catapults,made from forked sticks and elastic, peashooters,from hollowed out plant stems to go with our wooden swords,made from to pieces of wooden baton nailed together.Once "armed" we would dress up to play out imaginary battles.Plaster of paris figures turned out of red rubber moulds and painted to grace the bedroom window sills.Paper snowflakes and little rows of paper dolls to hang from the ceiling with wool..Airfix model kits glued together and painted,badly,using little tins of Humbrol enamel paint,with a tiny paintbrush, necklaces made from the contents of the button tin,empty glass bottles covered in plaster of paris then seashells picked up from the beach added to make vases and lamps.

Tired out,I would eat my tea,listening to Uncle Mac,Larry the Lamb and Dennis the Dachshund in Toytown and then clear up before bed.putting all the toys away,ready to get out again the following morning,
Where was the computer?........exactly there wasn't one.Ironically without one you wouldn't be reading this......but what made you happiest reading these memories or sat motionless at a desk looking at a screen!

++

 Cycle rides were great adventures in themselves when I was just a kid..Up and out in the early mornings with my old khaki rucksack on my back, filled with jam sandwiches,jam tarts and a bottle of lemonade I made my way through what today would be termed a rush hour.This comprised of mostly bikes but the odd car or too.It was like bees in a swarm as the factories up the Fareham Road filled with their workers....Osmiroid,Ultra,Fleetlands Royal Navy Aircraft Yard and the Provincial bus station at Hoeford.
Joined by a couple of pals we would cycle on regardless, in more danger of falling off than being knocked off,soon we passed the Tom Parker's Dairy on the junction of. Newgate Lane before continuing on to the creek at Fareham.If the tide was out the smell was"unique" and yachts would be resting on the mudflats.awaiting the incoming tide.At the end of the narrow channel skirting the beds of marine grass and sea lavender was tethered a dirty scruffy collier disgorging its coal cargo into Corralls yard in time for it to catch the next tide and return to sea to steam up the English Channel to Newcastle to gather its next cargo.The epitome of John Masefield's,"Dirty British coaster with a salt-caked smoke stack".
 On under the railway viaduct,shrouded in steam as one of the various goods trains headed towards Fareham Station,we proceeded up to the main A27,unrecognisable today by its lack of traffic.Right turn,past the fire station to the traffic lights at the Red Lion hotel,gazed longingly at

the cake shop and turned left up the hill.A brief stop at the sweet shop to spend our one old penny or two old pennies ,then on up the hill to turn right down the road that ran alongside the River Wallington.So quiet you could almost hear a pin drop but in fact the silence was broken,not by a pin but by water voles dropping into the water,or kingfishers diving for minnows.Oh how I long for the days before pollution when the water was vibrant and teemed with life.

 Going up a long drawn out hill,the last few yards usually on foot as the bikes with five speed Sturmey Archer gears weren't that efficient.I rested at the top and then freewheeled down past Boarhunt church, rounding the bend to the busy farmyard.Years later this farm was devastated by foot and mouth but these times were happier the byres with clean hay full of black and white cattle.We sat next to the pond with its resident ducks and moorhen and ate our lunches often surrounded by winged and noisy beggars with webbed feet clamouring to join in and share.

 Refreshed we cycled on through the bluebell woods,past the farm cottages to join up with the road that led back up to the top of Portsdown Hill.At this junction sat an ancient farmhand pulling on a pipe as he milked a solitary cow by hand.He acknowledged us as we leant on the gate,beckoning us in,so we entered into the field to watch as he part filled a shining steel pail.He said very little but invited us to partake of the warm milk,passing us a small tin cup.To this day I have never tasted sweeter or creamier milk....it tasted of the meadow that the cow grazed from,a taste no more found as the flora laden pastures now are bare of the nectar laden wildflowers,they only have one plant.....grass!!

 Wistfully we said farewell,turned and made our way from the meadow,cycling wearily over the route we had arrived on,grateful for the long free wheel down into Wallington.I,very tired,made my way back to home,slower than I had started out that morning but no less enthusiastic... full of my adventure and happiness.

Saturday lunch was often egg and chips and in the winter when eaten it was the signal to fill a flask with tea, make a small packet of paste sandwiches and off we would go to Privett Park with Nan to watch "the Boro" play football.Rain, hail or wind we would go and sit in the cold wooden stand next to where the players came out,Nana and I with a blanket over our legs it was so bitterly cold. Mr Stan Bray was the club chairman,always smartly dressed in a navy blue blazer and complete with scarf and wooden rattle,he would loudly shout "come on the BORO",deafening all around him.

The summer would see us in the same park watching cricket and sometimes Dad would walk up there with Rastus the golden retriever,mostly on finer winter days when football was in season as he did like chasing a cricket ball.The dog was so big I could ride on his back,with hindsight not a clever thing, and was so obedient with a capital "O".In fact one day he was told to sit on the side of the football pitch,whilst Dad moved up and down the touchline watching the game.When the game ended he was far enough away from his dog and forgot he had taken him and went home.On arriving home he realised when no dog arrived to greet him what he had done,quickly he returned after probably about forty-five minutes Rastus was still waiting,obediently and fortuitously where he had been left.

Other afternoons found us heading to the seaside, or at least Stokes Bay or Gilkicker Point.This journey took one of several routes.It could be we walked down to The White Hart and then followed the old railway line,the disused track now removed,all that was left, a shingle path past John Hunts builders yard and then across Alver Creek.We normally stopped off to see if we could see any crabs or dabs in the water and then continued to the sea shore along the old historical line.Sometimes we would take another route past the old Haslar cemetery and Baileys piggery,down to Haslar sea wall to watch the water crash against the wall and the paddle steamers wend their route to the Isle of Wight However if the tide was out we would walk along the edge of the creek past the clumps of sea lavender and turn up past the National Children's Home buildings crossing over the road and down towards the beach,passing the old decaying Victorian pier,following past Gilkicker point and onto the shingle beach.I would pass the time looking for little ringed plover nests on the shingle beach or farther inland,bordering the golf course, skylarks nests in the tussocky grass.Two very different birds but in one way very much the same as they were very skilled in landing and leading you away from their nests.In amongst the stones grew yellow horned poppies,samphire and blue extremely prickly sea holly.

 A quick scout along the shore line for shells and any cuttlefish that had been washed up,the white chalky skeleton was ideal when washed for the cage birds to sharpen their beaks on.The smell of it being washed in a pan of hot water,not the most pleasant, was supposedly justified in its use....I think it was most likely a ploy to get us to bed early.

++

 Supermarkets were virtually unheard of until they arrived from America in the late 60's.Self service was almost unheard of and the most common of self service places nowadays,the petrol station,was a very different experience to modern days.As you went up Forton Road from the Criterion,at the Crossways you came upon Hutfield and Wheelers garage.The brick offices,sited to the side of the main forecourt,homed the coach tour operation,numerous blackboards stood outside colourfully chalked on with the names of just as colourful destinations.Daily "charabanc" trips would export you to the New Forest,Bognor Regis,or Goodwood Races,alternatively a week's holiday in Torquay.Alongside this was the car showroom and workshops fronted by the petrol station.On the forecourt stood single pumps topped with illuminated glass advertising globes,Mobil,Esso,Shell,Castrol,shining brightly once daylight had turned to night.All the fuel was dispensed by an elderly attendant.who also energetically cleaned your windscreen and lights whilst asking if"you needed any air" and was ready to check your oil if it was required..

  This brings me back to the lack of supermarkets.Every shop was run by a tradesman well versed in the goods they sold,as was the attendant dispensing the fuel..Every little shop had its own expert relied on heavily to give advice on the items housed within them,no matter what it was.Mr Jones the butcher in Whitworth Road could advise what cuts were best for what type of cooking.I remember the joints on the counter on which was pinned a paper ticket showing the weight and price, which when selected was re-weighed in case the weight had changed due to it having dried out.Once purchased you paid the lady sat behind the glass screen in the little office in the corner of the shop.The same happened at Arnetts and Hoopers the fishmongers who would clean and fillet the fish for you,without being asked after you had selected your purchase based on their advice and knowledge.of the best catch that day.At various shops,Liptons,International Stores and the Maypole you could sample the cheese to gauge how strong they were particularly the cheddars.Other regional varieties were available,caerphilly,cheshire,lancashire,wensleydale and stilton but foreign cheese comprising of gouda.edam.gorgonzola.danish blue,and camembert were beginning to pick up in popularity and that was about all that was readily available.Dyers dairy shops still patted butter,impressed with a fancy pattern and served in a greaseproof paper wrap,ceramic milk pails still lined the white marbled counter at the rear of the shop..

 Add to this the bakers shops like Greens and Smith& Vospers, where cut bread was the exception but the range of crusty bread a feast to the eyes.

There were cottage,finger,bridge and vienna rolls,displayed in large wicker baskets,small tins.long tins small and large farmhouse,small and large bloomers,coburgs,milk loaves and my favourite the cottage loaf,all waiting to be liberally buttered after being sliced at home to the thickness required.
Aagh I rue the demise of those old wooden breadboards and bread knives!! but not the cut fingers!!

++

When sweets came off rationing they were still in short supply largely due to sugar remaining on ration till September,later that year,However the Dugout, in Lees Lane was a local sweet shop,just along from Chiltern Grove,the site of the old prison,a nice little shop, although the little sweet shop in Whitworth Road opposite the old Central School was my favourite.Entering the door,as it opened, a bell rang hanging above it alerting the lady who owned it,in fact it was the front room of her house.My eyes filled with awe at the rows of glass jars with metal lids filled with all manner of sweet delights.They were all sold loose,weighed by the quarter,four ounces, but you could buy as little as an ounce,or ask for one or two penneth.These sweets were weighed out on a small set of scales with a silver scoop,brass weights providing the measure,then they were poured into a white paper bag. What a choice of sweets there was,,,pear drops,can always remember their distinctive smell,,aniseed balls,pontefract cakes,jelly beans,wine gums,tom thumb drops to name but a few. I can always remember teacakes,nothing remotely to do with buns.tiger nuts presumably not connected to tigers, and liquorice root.Gob stoppers filled your mouth and kept you quiet for hours and liquorice laces and cartwheels turned your mouth black. If only a penny to spend you could get four or eight mojos,blackjacks or fruit salad chews or even for that penny a bar of Cadbury's milk chocolate in its distinctive purple wrapper! Cartons of

Black Magic,Dairy Box and Milk Tray were sold in half pound boxes bought for only extremely special occasions as were items like Callard and Bowser cherry nougat,montelimar, and liquid centred New Berry Fruits from Meltis As the 1950's progressed the varieties available increased but one item that remained forever and never changed was the silver tray of Bluebird toffee complete with a little silver hammer to break it up!. With all that no wonder the school dentist was always busy down the bottom of Spring Garden Lane.That awful drill powered by the dentist's foot and with a drill the size of a modern Black & Decker,it's no surprise many people ended up with dentures from that era.

++

 Mothering Sunday 1950's style almost certainly incorporated a visit to church with the whole family.On returning,everyone pitched in to prepare dinner and then have a family afternoon playing board games,ludo,draughts,snakes and ladders,the adults enjoying cribbage,shove ha'penny or dominoes or if it was a fine day maybe a leisurely stroll..
 No dinners at overpriced restaurants,no expensive presents of chocolate and wine,no extravagant gestures stored up to make an impression,cheap considered gifts with often no financial outlay at all. a simple bunch of daffodils or flowers plucked from the hedgerow or garden,a simple hand made card crafted,coloured and inscribed with love and meaning.
 Maybe a few twigs of catkins,pussy willow or even early primroses and violets would make up a bouquet that mother would be proud to receive,even if it was at times rather bedraggled or imperfect.

 One thing for sure the naivety and simplicity was truly meant as a genuine appreciation of what mum did for you all year......until commercial greed took it away and keeping up with others became fashionable....

++

Make do and mend...exactly what it said. If it was broken you repaired it, if you couldn't repair it and couldn't afford a replacement you went without until you could, more often than not the replacement would be a second or third hand purchase even when you could afford it. The knife sharpener would sharpen knives and mowers until they were too thin to do anything with, the odd "Irish" tinker would call and offer to repair saucepans until there were more holes than metal. Bicycle tyres would be repaired, the inner tube removed, immersed in a bowl of water and the hole identified by the rising stream of tiny bubbles, then using yellow crayon from the repair kit to mark the spot a rubber patch was glued in place, chalk dust sprinkled on to make sure it never stuck to the tyre.
If a broom broke you fitted a new handle, the old handle adapted to make a "dibber" for the allotment, if a hoe, fork or spade broke a blacksmith could help out although they were starting to become a scarce sight.
 If the washing line broke you tied it together again, until it was too short to tie the knot anymore, if the fuse blew in a plug then you fixed it with the wire which was purchased from Mr Clogg's hardware shop in Whitworth Road wrapped around a cardboard card.
 However it was clothes which mostly were given the repair treatment. All families would pass clothes down from older to younger children until they simply wore out, fit for only the rag and bone man. Old bonnets were rejuvenated with a ribbon or flower, woollen jumpers were picked apart and reworked if they couldn't be patched. Socks and ladies woollen stockings would be darned. Patches were added to the knees of trousers and patches of leather were sewn on the elbows and cuffs of favourite jackets

Buttons,hooks and eyes were a must for the button tin,zips were removed from old clothes,recycled and reused to replace broken ones,even if the wrong colour at times,as were buttons which as long as they were close enough to the original they would.

The final piece of equipment was the shoe last which was used to repair shoes and knock nails flat when they sometimes worked their way through the leather soles.New rubber soles were stuck over the worn leather ones ,cardboard was cut to shape and put inside the shoe to cover holes and stop the leaks,Shoe laces were sometimes the wrong colour but more often than not they were tied back together if they had snapped.

++

After the second world war,in fact well into the nineteen fifties, many foodstuffs were still scarce,subsequently, the concept of not wasting or throwing away any useful item was important in putting food on our table.All homes used their leftovers to supplement the daily meals or simply as a basis for another days meal but nothing was wasted,it had a use for something..

Uneaten food may have been used to feed the chickens,dogs and cats were fed on table scraps and biscuit,ready "complete" feeds were simply not available.Meat bones were used for stock and soup,cooked but unused vegetables used for delicious bubble and squeak.Fallen bruised fruit would have "the brown pieces cut out" and used for the basis of puddings,pies and jams..

I can remember chickens in the old corrugated tin and wire hen run at the back of the garden,they were raised on a kind of porridge made of meal,which had a far from unpleasant smell, and vegetable peelings,fattening up for the Christmas table,They were an assortment of pullets and bantams,Rhode Island Reds or Wyandottes and as well as the festive dinner they were also kept for their eggs.Too many eggs, and the surplus were immersed in isinglass water,to preserve them,placed in a large earthenware crock pot to keep them fresh for the leaner times of winter.

There were no freezers and the methods of keeping produce were really rather primitive but effective.Grandad used to grow far more vegetables than needed and root vegetables in particular were preserved by burying in a hay lined clamp to keep them over winter, strings of sun dried onions were plaited,then hung in the shed.Other vegetables like runner beans,saw the green Spong slicer come out and when sliced packed in salt, in airtight Kilner jars for the winter.Soft fruit was put in the same type of glass jars immersed in sugar syrup for use in pies and tarts,or if too soft made into jams preserves and even chutneys Apples and pears were individually wrapped in newspaper,sometimes placed in sand,but only if unblemished,before placing in wooden crates in a cool dry place in the garden shed.those that were turned into jams.chutneys and pickles smelt divine when cooking.They were placed in reused,warmed jars,cooled once filled, before covering with a greaseproof circle and cloth top secured with string or elastic band.]

I remember the outings to pick blackberries for pies and jams,equipped with the obligatory walking stick to pull the branches down,also picking of red rose hips to make syrup and rose petals to make scented water.

Herbs,thyme,sage,rosemary and mint, were tied in bunches and dried in the scullery,hanging from the ceiling airer, we used them to make sage and onion stuffing,subtle flavourings,When fresh,raw horseradish,dug from the hedgerow went with roast beef,apple sauce made to accompany pork,fresh mint added to vinegar and sugar to have with the lamb.Even mustard was made from powder!

The baker on his rounds often had a cheap stale loaf which would provide breadcrumbs or even the basis of a very welcome bread pudding.

Nothing was wasted, as if anything was past eating, even if the mould had been scraped off, the pigman would come round with his horse and cart and take it away to use for pig food or swill.

++

Winters were pretty harsh and every penny was put to good use to make them more comfortable and bearable.The weekly Sunday visits to Ann's Hill Cemetery supplied us with additional wood for the fire, which we picked up from the fallen branches brought down by the winds.It was vital to keep warm and the elderly and young were at risk in the cold damp houses,central heating and double glazing only a futuristic dream.Regularly when you woke in the mornings the inside of the windows were decorated with icy patterns even after we had crammed old newspaper into the gaps and crevices to stop the draughts.You woke up to cold...real cold.The hot water bottles became so cold they had been kicked out of bed during the night.The coal fire was lit as soon as Nana arose so at least we could huddle around it with a hot drink,usually milk sometimes with sugar added, until a hot bowl of porridge appeared on the table,I can still smell the burnt milk as it had boiled over;A quick wash with water boiled on the gas stove from a kettle which seemed to constantly be whistling to signal it had boiled and dress in lukewarm clothes hung on the wooden clothes horse in front of the now roaring fire.

By now outside the yellow fog had begun to thicken,the smog as it was called due to the high amount of smoke in it,enveloped everywhere,it pervaded the lungs,so it was important to wear not only gloves and a balaclava helmet but a thick scarf wrapped around your mouth and throat to prevent you inhaling the freezing polluted air.

Chest infections and tuberculosis were still major killers at the time and polio,chicken pox.mumps.measles and scarlet fever were major diseases and killers in the young.

People in general only lived,if they were lucky for three score and ten and anyone older than that was revered,in fact was as ancient as the mariner in Coleridge's poem..If you lived long enough to get a telegram,delivered by the lad on his General Post Office Telegraph motorbike with a greeting from the queen you became an overnight celebrity or even made a saint!

The upside of course to this winter wonderland was the ice thick enough on the ponds to walk on,to skate on at Gosport Boating lake and then the snow which fell every year.The icicles on roofs and gutters,heavily snow laden branches looking like something from a Victorian Christmas were like magic.The wooden toboggans.snowballs and tribe of snowmen appeared in every back and front garden.Each white glistening figure complete with a small piece of coal for nose and eyes,carrots were not to be wasted as they were food, his arms made from twigs.

Was I unhappy then...no way you took the "rough with the smooth" and I was too busy enjoying myself with pals outdoors.If I close my eyes I can hear the shrieks,squeals.laughing,shouting and sometimes the odd cry,as a cold snowball hit uncovered skin of the hapless target.Sometimes even the harshest days were fun and I wouldn't change a thing.

++

That enigmatic shed in the garden.Time after time I returned to that shed to peer through the crack in the door,it was always secured with a large iron padlock,the key hidden out of sight and reach.Although I say shed, it was more of a "Heath Robinson" affair made from salvaged wood and actually split into two parts.The half which was always unlocked was the uninteresting coal bunker.Inside the door was a series of planks which slotted into the door frame depending on the amount of coal inside.Also there was a tin shovel and a large wire sieve which was used to sieve the larger pieces in the daily ash bucket to re-burn,waste not want not and every penny counted.

 The second half of the shed,however, was a virtual cornucopia of hidden treasures.To a young lad it was a veritable aladdin's cave.Inside the gloomy interior stood a mangle,lawn mower and tin bath,but it was the jars,,tins and bent nails, hammered into the wooden walls, that held the riches.There were hammers,wooden mallets,awls,augurs,bradles,pliers and various chisels and screwdrivers.There were various types of saws,even billhooks,scythes and sickles.The tins and jars held screws,old fashioned,hand made iron nails,hooks,washers,bits of metal and strips of leather all which"might come in useful one day" Other jars held paint brushes soaking,in turpentine,standing beside linseed oil,paraffin and various solvents,none labelled but common sense dictated you never drunk from them!!.In the corner stood two cases of stuffed birds somebody was throwing away and thought they might be something I would like.Various pieces of wood stood in the corner with bundles of pea and bean sticks,around the floor various gardening tools and the infamous besom broom.Stacked around the floor were various hemp sacks,and pieces of sisal and string.The piece de resistance was the pile of brittle glass stacked up against the corner of a wall in case we needed it[Why I ask myself]

 Health and Safety eat your heart out,commonsense was the forte of the day,mind your step,was the old adage.and you learnt by asking questions not blundering headlong into an abyss.You learnt to avoid the dangers by never exposing yourself to them.

+++

 Now that Easter was on its way it was time for the dreaded ritual of spring cleaning.Nobody could reek as much havoc as a head scarved lady complete with pinafore as Nana.If you stood still long enough,about ten seconds, you could be swept up and given any chore that needed a duster,the duster being an old vest or pair of long johns no longer wearable but clean.

 We would start at the front step,scrubbed daily but spring cleaning meant it got extra treatment and in some cases a treatment of "cardinal red" paint and polish.The door then got its yearly varnish and so we went on.The hallway went down to the living room and was covered in what looked like dark treacle paper half way up to the dado rail and then was wallpapered above.The runner in the hall along with all the rugs in the house,"fitted" carpets not being an option were carried out to the washing line,hung up and with the bamboo carpet beater beaten to within an inch of their lives! Whilst this took place all the muslin,lace curtains were boiled in the copper to wash out the nicotine which prevailed in most houses added to by the smoke from the open fires.Cushion covers,antimacassars and curtains were washed pressed and folded away into drawers and replaced with their summer counterparts.Even the drawers they were in had their linings replaced by the current copy of the "News Chronicle" and later by new synthetic Fablon.In between an obligatory handful of moth balls were tossed into every possible storage unit.

 The food cupboards had their turn next,they were treated similarly,fortunately minus the mothballs,although an odd mouse trap could be found from time to time lingering in their depths

 The beds, next, had the summer linen put on,the glass,gas light shades were washed,then dried and any walls, not papered, and all ceilings, were liberally coated in whitewash or distemper.

 The fireplaces up and downstairs were given the cardinal red treatment and metal grates treated with black lead and stood gleaming against the fenders and brass compendium sets.

 Every possible nook and cranny was dealt with by this elderly lady,with her conscripts, complete with a real feather duster on the longest bamboo cane you can imagine,it reached the very height of the stairs to remove cobwebs.She put The White Tornado to shame.God help

Grandad as if he didn't drink up his bottle stout quickly enough he would have been teetotal within the week.

++

Running along the back of the terraced houses in Leesland Road was an alleyway, dividing postage stamp sized gardens,think ours must have been second class it was so small, from those for the houses in Norman Road.However small it was it still contained an incredible amount.Apart from the scullery drain.,outside loo and the wooden and perforated zinc meat safe hanging on the brick wall, there was room for a shed incorporating a coal bunker.Once I had managed to edge past these obstacles I came to a small but neatly kept garden.

A flower bed ran down the left side,the fence and privet hedge separating it from that of Mrs King the neighbour, on the other boundary was a wire fence along which grew loganberries,blackberries and raspberries which during the summer provided the fruit for the Sunday pie or "tart" as Nana called it By the shed was another flower bed in which grew tagetes.gladioli,phlox,michaelmas daisy, dahlia and "esther reads".The later were large white daisies and for a long time I wondered why they grew in Nan's garden when they were Miss Reads who lived next door!

There was in the centre a small neat square of grass with an apple tree in the middle,yes, the one Grandad had hung from during an air raid during world war two,It was my chore to clip around the edges with what looked like sprung sheep shears whilst Nana pushed the light single cylinder mower to cut the grass.There was no grass box attached to the mower so grass cuttings were swept up with a besom broom,Nana's broomstick,then piled by the chicken house which was at the very back of the garden.The chickens,well that's another story, but fresh eggs and Christmas dinner would not have been the same without them.

++

Two seven letter words had shaped much of my life during the next two decades after the wartime years,being born in 1949 meant life was starting slowly to return to normality.
 Meal times in those days were very organised,very formal, starting with everybody washing their hands before eating,something which we will do well to remember in the future..Grace was said in most households,religion had a big influence, everybody waited for everyone else to be served before they started to eat.There was no talking with your mouth full,no elbows on the tables,no reaching across somebody to get the salt,no getting down from the table unless everyone had finished and then I had to ask,most importantly everything was performed with "please and thank you".'I spoke when spoken to,I was to be"seen but not heard".Seems strict..it was but it was the framework for society and gave me the foundations for my own life..no not really strict..just what was expected and needed.
 After the meal I could go out to play but I was expected to return at the agreed time,I was not expected to write graffiti on the walls or pavement,it didn't belong to me,I was trusted to comply with what was deemed acceptable.If you used a chalk to play hopscotch on the pavement,both boys and girls joined in,we were expected to clean it off when the game was over.
 Then,of course, there were people.If somebody dropped something you picked it up,if somebody fell you helped them up.,you certainly didn't laugh at their misfortune."Do as you would be done by",was the saying,it may well be you in the same predicament on a future occasion,needing their assistance .You helped elderly people across the road,you stepped aside,giving room pass without having to step into the roadway.you gave up your seat on the bus to your elders and you put everybody before yourself.Elderly people were

respected,assisted and not ignored,their wisdom revered as they had had full lives and much experience.This was how we learnt.You queued and awaited your turn when in a shop,if they had sold out when your turn came you accepted it as just being unfortunate,next time you made sure you were earlier in the queue,you didn't shout at the shopkeeper and give a tirade of abuse as if your misfortune was their fault.
 Sorry meant just that,excuse me was polite,thank you and please were the normal
.

OH... and the two seven letter words?....MANNERS and RESPECT!!

++

 Desserts,or puddings as I would rather call them,were a necessity before I would leave the table at lunchtime,they were designed,not to make us fat but to encourage people from snacking,eating between meals was unnecessary.Ice cream fetched from the "stop me and buy one"Walls Ice Cream man on his tricycle was a rare treat in the warm summer months.We could get a bowl of icecream,one of Nana's pudding bowls, for a few pence and this would be served with an Askeys wafer or occasionally a Barmouth biscuit..On special days we may have sterilised cream from a tin of "Carnation" evaporated milk poured onto a Rowntrees or Hartley's fruit jelly .This could be augmented by a Brown and Poulsons blancmange ,if there was no money it would be DIY,a blancmange made with cornflour and vanilla essence.Another sweet treat was Fussells condensed milk,so delicious I could eat it by the spoonful!!.... Normally it was eaten at breakfast time instead of treacle on the morning porridge, or spread on bread for a teatime treat,Tea nearly always had cake of some kind,mostly homemade and simple,madeira,cherries added were a luxury,victoria sponge or desiccated coconut cake..

Even a biscuit was given as a treat,rarely given during the day but often at bedtime,referred to as being suppertime,to accompany a mug of Horlicks,Ovaltine or Cocoa before we went up the wooden hill to the Land of Nod.

My thoughts often linger back to the gloriously "unhealthy" foods I was fed with in the lean years of rationing, before they were fully lifted in 1955.When I was growing up the whole of any animal,killed for meat was eaten not just "the best cuts",the steak.I was more likely to have pigs trotters,pigs cheek, lamb or ox tongue,chaps,haslet and brawn along with heart,kidney,liver,chitterling or sweetbreads,but the best item of all[ugh] tripe and onions stewed in milk.

What delicacies they were, finished off by cooking in dripping,lard,and butter, as oil and margarine were still relatively additions,from memory Stork,Cooken and Summer County margarines where the first] for cooking.Fish was generally coley,mackerel,sprats,cod or haddock,skate and cod or herring roe was a treat,salmon,trout and scampi almost unheard of.John Wests tinned red,or the cheaper pink, salmon was for high days and holidays!

All this fat,it was not sufficient to cook with it,it was eaten on bread,not the lard, that was used to fry the bread,but beef dripping on toast,and toast or crusty bread spread with fresh butter was heaven..

Roly poly pudding,spotted dick,suet pudding, bread pudding and bread and butter pudding,all served with liberal helpings of home made Birds vanilla custard.They were all made to "fill you up" as portions were smaller then than today,"seconds" rarely available.As an extra,the cream from the gold top milk was served with tinned peaches,pears or fruit salad when condensed milk was not affordable,full cream milk was used to make rice,macaroni,sago,semolina and tapioca pudding,all from the dry grains..Meat portions were small,meat was expensive,fresh vegetables were served everyday,mostly grown on the family allotment but added to from Mr Shepherds vegetable cart..Dumplings would supplement the meat in a stew, bread and butter often added to eke out the meals and "soak up the gravy".

All of this frugality but I always seem to have had enough.The extra fat was burnt off during our high energy games in the playgrounds or in the street after school and I was constantly active.on the go.

 The school photographs of the era show very few overweight children and many of my generation are now part of the ever-ageing population which is living longer than ever before..Some of us are slightly wider and slower but only really since the advent of processed food and ready meals,coupled with less activity and more sedentary hobbies and pastimes.! That unhealthy diet certainly seems to have served us well and I would happily return to it tomorrow.

 It was all so simple,so acceptable and our childhood was one of readily being normal,we were the same, like everyone around us,we were equals to one another and consequently we tolerated each other far better
.We had all or nothing together.

++

 On the inevitable wet days during the school holidays it was always a challenge which not always meant staying in,it was not comfortable getting wet but sometimes inevitable.Life continued,holiday or not,with no refrigeration most fresh food was purchased almost daily,getting wet was a small price to pay. Often dressed in wellington boots,yellow sou'wester and mackintosh we would venture out for a walk,to the shops ,even to the cemetery and football fans to football matches always secure in the knowledge that there would be a roaring coal fire and hot buttered crumpets toasted over the said fire.for tea.

 A little rain,or even occasionally a torrential downpour did little to dampen the spirits but if it did we could always entertain ourselves indoors.the gloom made cheerful by the laughter inside.

Board games were a sure fire winner,ludo.snakes and ladders.and hoopla,or card games with Mr Bun the Baker and company, or simple Snap whiled away the time.Cooking of jam tarts,or fairy cakes,complete with icing,hundreds and thousands and silver dragees were a good standby and meant an extra treat for tea,regardless of some very odd shapes they tasted good,if sometimes a little burnt.

There was in every house the obligatory pad of paper,crayons and colouring pencils in addition to tracing paper,greaseproof paper from the kitchen, so we could copy our favourite pictures,then colour them in..At certain times we were lucky enough to have had a plastic Airfix Kit of a plane,car or boat bought for us which we glued together along with our fingers.and in the loosest meaning of the word, "painted" them with little tins of Humbrol enamel paints.

No money, so we made do with free materials, papier mache bowls made from newspaper and glue made of flour and water then painted with poster paints mixed up from powder. Sometimes plaster of paris models were made in red rubber moulds,left to dry before painting,to be given as presents.

One toy we made puzzles me even today... made from a used cotton reel.spent matchsticks,elastic bands and a "washer" of a circle of wax cut from a candle.When assembled this managed to travel across the ground but for what purpose...no idea!!

Supposedly it was meant to be a model tank but I needed a very vivid imagination to see any resemblance to the real thing.

++

Summer holidays were full of excitement,anticipation and adventure,but with very little money imagination was needed to keep me and my friends occupied,

This imagination started at home and had to be fitted around an already busy day,all the activity was on top of what had to be done as normal.

Thus,it was,I found myself complete with a well laden pushchair travelling the lane between the cemetery and Southcroft Road up to the Military Road.It was always hot and the sky seemed to be endlessly sunny, blue and cloudless as passed the entrance to what was to become H M S Sultan before turning right along the track which eventually led to Browndown.In the mid 1950.s the old Grange Airfield stood almost deserted ,except in one corner where there was a compound full of damaged planes,Walking past this Nana and I took the dusty track through the gorse bushes,checking for red flags as we crossed the military firing range and headed towards our destination of the stream and Apple Dumpling Bridge.The rickety wooden bridge over the River Alver had been a crossing for hundreds of years and possibly was the site of a disused ford.On arriving I would paddle my feet in the clean crystal clear water or lay face down and peer in the stream.listening to the sound of wild bird song.Our paste sandwiches,beef,chicken, shrimp and even bloater,were unwrapped from their greaseproof paper packages and along with a slice of swiss roll and home made lemonade or ginger beer we sat and had a picnic.The area was alive with the swallows,skylarks and yellowhammers or the odd flash of a kingfisher to be seen as it hurried to capture the minnows and sticklebacks before us.

Lunch over,out came the fishing net,purchased for threepence,just a long bamboo handle the two wire ends pressed into the top of the cane.Alongside the net was accompanied by a jam jar with a string handle attached to it in which we could carry any prisoners home.Unfortunately we had no idea how to keep them alive and after a

few short days they met a tragic end.fish or tadpoles their demise was always the same....inevitable death.

After what seemed all day the pushchair was loaded up, often now with one of us,me or my sister, incumbent,unable to walk any further as we wove our weary path home
Did we sleep well that night....yes, but what an adventure to dream about and tell the world the next day!

++

Following on from the scrubbing of the doorstep,polishing the brass door knocker and sweeping of the pavement....YES the women swept the pavement with coarse bristle yard brooms each day,the welcome was ready for the days visitors.Trust was a great thing as people let themselves into neighbours houses, the doors were always open and tradesmen just walked in to leave their goods,even when you weren't there.
Well these people were frequent visitors and they needed you to earn a living so they needed to be trustworthy.
The Co-op baker in his brown coat with a selection of various uncut loaves,cut bread was virtually unheard of, in a large wicker basket carried over his arm would just walk in,his colleague the Co-op grocer would enter with his box of pre-ordered groceries placing them on the dining table.The Corona man with his bottles of "pop",stacked in crates on his yellow Commer lorry, even the coalman with a hessian sack of coal on his shoulder would walk through to deposit the said coal in the coal shed in the backyard.
Other people that arrived in the road included,the ice-cream man and his trike displaying"stop me and buy one",in the winter it might be the hot chestnut man with his cart and brazier,the chestnuts put in a little white paper bag.The knife grinder with his grindstone which he operated with a foot treadle,the rag and bone man recycling much that would be thrown today and my favourite the Romanies, the true gypsies.They would walk up the road from door to door followed by the

very ornate horse drawn caravans.They were usually old ladies with head scarves and shawls, in their wicker baskets hung over their arms were wooden pegs,lucky white heather and ribbons,They would ask you to"cross my palm with silver" and in return they would wish you good luck.

 The one thing these people had in common that they openly carried amounts of money with them but I don't remember any one being tempted to mug or rob them.It was very much each to his own and what was "yours was yours" and "what was theirs was theirs"!!!!! If only now!

++

 Telephones were few and far between in houses after the war years so we relied heavily on the red boxes at the street corners with their heavy black phones and coin boxes telling us to push button A and then button B.Quite often after doing that the money came back out into a little silver coin cup and you started all over again!.Each kiok also contained a telephone directory,for some reason a mirror and a place to display "business" cards,sometimes of dubious origins.The kiosks were cleaned daily by a smart man on a bike who collected the money from the coin boxes,as well as cleaning,these phone boxes either smelt of Jeyes fluid or stale urine and cigarette smoke depending on whether he had been or not..

 Thinking of these red boxes my mind wandered to the other arm of the General Post Office the postman who was the deliverer of either bills,family news,yes,we really did write letters then,and everyone sent thank you letters for their birthday or christmas cards,or greetings or postcards[if you were able to afford to go away on holiday!]......the one thing not there was any junk mail !!

 We listened to the daily news on the little bakelite radio which broadcasted the Home or Light service,using short,medium or long waves unless you were lucky enough to own one of the new fangled televisions.

Newspapers heralded news that sometimes due to the time scale was old before we got to read it,in fact more history by the time it reached us,really the majority of our news,especially local, was delivered by that strange skill we used to have of talking.Everyone knew everyone and news items were relayed down the road faster than a modern telephone!

Neighbours were your friends and seen to support one another,your link with the community,whereas in modern life you may as well live on an island.It wasn't seen as being nosey but caring and looking out for one another.

++

Well,depression was not an option growing up,it wasn't a word that tended to trip off the tongue,it was more likely to be "let's look at the bright side of life".There was so much nature to see,so many sights,smells and sounds to enjoy,all of it free,abundantly available to everyone.

Maybe it was because we didn't spend our time trying to be better or have more than someone else,the fact,the reality was that adventure knowledge and life itself filled our childhood days.

We learnt about fauna and flora and what life meant by experiencing it,We went pond dipping,fishing with little threepenny nets and jam jars,we knew the life of a stickleback because we experienced it.We went butterfly catching,we hunted wild flowers and knew the migration of swallows,could tell the seasons and weather from nature and its forms.Many of the old sayings had meaning and were based on facts which are now long forgotten.

Well I hope this doesn't depress too many of you as to me these memories and nostalgia only give me reason to celebrate and give thanks for a childhood that was so rewarding.How simple life was when we considered others and had time for everybody,not just ourselves!

++

How many of my 1950's peers remember the "echoes of silence" when silence was really golden! No constant hum or buzz of background noise wherever you venture.The chance to wake to the dawn chorus,the call of the cuckoo or the fading nocturnal warble of a distant nightingale,none of it drowned by the constant drone of an engine,a radio or some other mechanised abomination..
 You could ride a bicycle or even walk to deserted fields near Rowner Lane and there you could revel in that idyll of those sounds which made up that sought after silence.
 You could lay yourself down in a lush green field devoid of pesticides and smell and hear the silence.The smell of grass, wet or dry,the smell of the manure on the field ,the smell of the soil,and the smell of fresh raindrops on dry pavements.
 Most of all was that this silence was made up of the sounds which modern living drowns out.The plop of the water vole into the stream,the constant buzz and hum of winged insects,the rustle of a lizard in the grass,the song of the skylark high up almost invisible in the azure blue sky.Rooks would caw from the rookery and water would splash silently as it ran its course over rocks and pebbles, then be joined by the rustling movement of a mouse or rabbit in the long dry grass.
 Occasionally a horse would whinny,a cow moo or a lamb bleat and the only noises were the rare sound of a propeller driven aeroplane as it slowly made its way home,or an ancient tractor ploughing the field,in some places not even that,as horses were still used to till the land.A deafening silence which nobody will possibly ever enjoy again and was music to my ears.

Well Sunday came around quickly again,but after our grave duties we sometimes had a few minutes to spare so we walked down from Ann's Hill Cemetery to Wilmott Lane,to peer in the florists on the corner,located almost opposite the car lot on the opposite side of the road.We regularly wandered up Wilmott Lane passed the council depot,opposite the cemetery,where they stored the dustcarts and street sweeper's hand carts.The dustcarts which I think were Fodens and maroon in colour had sliding side covers which raised up and were then lowered to cover the rubbish.I can recall the dustbin men coming to collect the contents of the single metal dustbin,outside every door,no black sacks and due to the recycling mentality rarely full..Packaging was used very little,most items were sold loose,then just decanted into your shopping bag, the rag and bone man took most recyclables,anything metal,bone,rags or paper.Leftover food and vegetable peelings were made into a mash to feed the chickens by mixing with a corn meal purchased from Dittman & Malpass when we went to town,to shop,on Thursdays,Old clothes,if wool,were unpicked and re-knitted into another garment,cotton clothes were used as polishing clothes,even the fire ashes were used in the garden,or in winter put on the icy paths as it was cheaper than buying salt. Tins of course were used for storage as were screw top jars and glass bottles that had deposits so you wanted your money back.
  The smaller hand propelled carts in the depot were a similar design as their larger counterparts and were used by the road sweepers.I remember that we walked on up to Privet Park.to sit on the grass in the sun and watch the cricket teams immaculately dressed in their "whites",some probably more of a shade of cream.
  At tea they retired to a tea pavilion in the centre of the park.surrounded by evergreen hedges and as we looked longingly through the windows they partook in a veritable feast of ham,cheese,fish or meat paste

sandwiches,spread from little glass Shippams jars,fairy cakes and cups of tea.
 Having eaten well they returned to the crease with less spring in their legs than when they had originally left the field,a certain languidness in the warm sum,the soporific effect of the tea impinging on their concentration.Often a steady fall of wickets after tea so the result of a match change direction somewhat

++

 One very dark wet and windy night in the late 1950's a devastating whirlwind hit Alverstoke one night,its centre seemed to be located in the region of a small ancient graveyard on the corner of The Avenue and the road leading past St Mary's Church.Such was the force of
the wind that it tore up some large old trees,resulting in them being uprooted from the soft sodden soil,as their roots pulled out of the ground they uncovered some skeletal remains,The far reaching roots of the trees had the effect of bringing to the surface various bones belonging to long dead ancestors,much to the shock of passers by.I seem to recollect the edge of the graveyard bordered ontoThe Avenue on the opposite side of the road to the church.The recovery of the human remains was swift and resulted in them being re-interred,but the dislodged gravestones were placed against the wall around the boundaries of the sanctified ground.

++

 Whilst sat here having my lunch I began to remember about the hooter sounding to mark the start of each lunch hour at Ashleys,later Sandersons,wallpaper factory in Lees Lane,opposite the long disused prison in Chilworth Grove.Those that lived close scuttled home for dinner,others scuttled for liquid refreshment at The Junction or a packet of chips from the fish and chip shop in Whitworth Road.I remember the regular lunchtime radio show"Workers Playtime',broadcast from a works canteen "somewhere in the country".It was on three times a week and featured many celebrity artistes of the era.It was another legacy from wartime when it was used as a morale booster to industrial workers.In the evenings I would listen to Wilfred Pickles and his wife in the radio programme "Have a go Joe",and his catchphrases"give him the money Barney" and "what's on the table Mabel"

++

After school on a Friday I would walk up Whitworth Road to the Lees Lane railway crossing hoping to glimpse the steam locomotive hauling its wagons up to Fareham station..Those were the days when the old crossing keeper,Percy, came down from his signal box to open and close the heavy railway gates by hand.I would then go down Lees Lane past The Dugout where I might be lucky enough to have some sweets bought for me on the way back!.However on the way out Nana and I proceeded past the old prison site opposite the wallpaper factory and where the road forked took the right turn around the back of the "fleapit',or more politely The Criterion Cinema,then down past St John's school.Next to the school there was a piece of grass wasteland,which stood in front of St Johns Church and on the next corner could be found Croslands flower shop and undertakers, beside it the Chapel of Rest attached to his undertakers.At first there used to be a horse drawn hearse,which stood outside i but can remember the large gleaming black Armstrong Siddeley and Daimler limousines that replaced them in the mid 50's.Walking on past the playing fields which were used by HMS St Vincent was a small terrace of three or four shops and it was the first of these that we had come to visit.
 The owner was a short slightly dumpy man who wore black rimmed glasses, his hair was receding but what was left was slicked back and

he always had a cigarette in his mouth,which he removed and held in two fingers when he spoke to you..He wore a white waist length overall and when we opened the door you were met with the unmistakable odour of hair oil.Yes we had arrived for our "short back and sides", at the barbers traditionally advertised by the red and white pole outside.The chair was like a wooden armchair and a board was placed across the arms for me to sit on to bring me up to the right height.A white cloth was placed around my shoulders,his cigarette dangling from his lips,before he removed it,placed it in a glass ashtray and started to cut my hair.A quick snip here,a quick snip there with the scissors,it was all over in minutes,as the razor cut the back and sides to the required length.The hair clippings were flicked away with a soft haired brush,the neck powdered,the obligatory hair oil, which he rubbed between his hands,spread over the newly cut hair,before it was combed into place complete with a parting to one side.The mirror was then held up behind your head,"alright Nan" he would say, sixpence changed hands, and away we went heading for sweets possibly and sometimes a treat of egg and home made chips for tea!

++

I must have been about seven when emergency service vehicles had bells on their front bumpers ,they were rung in the event of attending an emergency.In those lazy days,vehicle speeds were relatively slow so you had plenty of time to get out of the way, in fact it was quite an event if a fire engine or ambulance came down the street.The whole neighbourhood came out to see the spectacle.
  Residents would watch in awe as an ancient fire engine disgorged its occupants who would run to roll out the hosepipe to nearby source.Their colleagues,hatchets tucked into their belts,would raise the"high rise"ladder by hand.Ambulances would arrive,with white coated staff and a stretcher,which was really no more than a

primitive canvas camp bed with a wooden pole either side with which to carry it.The vehicle that was viewed with some mystery,however was the "black Maria",a black Commer police van which would remove some character who had presumably committed an undetermined felony,his removal met with choruses of "I wonder what he's been up to."

++

 Close to Leesland Road,as you turned into Norman Road,next to Treloar's demolition yard,there stood a large white house which had begun to decay..It was fronted with a high metal rail fence and gates,the garden full of gnarled old fruit trees which increased the atmosphere of foreboding and it was reputed to be haunted.Although scary it was not sufficiently so as to stop us "scrumping" for apples on a warm evening.In fact it was such an evening that was to be my undoing.Having collected my rewards,from the finest red apples on the trees, I clambered up the fence,only to hear a deep voice say "got you" and as my feet touched the ground the heavy hand of the law,or rather the village bobby,foot patrol and bicycle were normal practice in those times,settled on my shoulder,before leading me home by the ear.In those days the local policeman knew where everybody on their beat lived.When we arrived on the doorstep of home we were greeted with a clip round the ear from the adult who opened the door,before anything was said whilst the bobby looked on approvingly.If the
policeman brought you home,unlikely you were lost but almost certainly guilty of some heinous crime,no innocent to proven guilty! No worry then about corporal punishment and it certainly did most of us no harm and taught us right from wrong.

++

I ventured into my first supermarket in the 1960's, in fact I started work in one in 1968, my memory slipped back to when my childhood shopping took place in corner shops or small specialising retail premises. A day out shopping for the weekly food supplies could take you into as many as ten shops, sometimes more. Everything was available in the supermarket, the Co-op being an early player but it was so impersonal, and nobody spoke. In post war times we could ask an expert. Mr Hooper or Mr Arnett the fishmonger would recommend the best value fish that particular day, the fish available being dependent on the seasons. Admittedly the range was limited, mainly the likes of haddock, cod, plaice, mackerel or herring, lemon sole and skate slightly more expensive but always fresh. Not available everyday but that was part of the attraction. Next would be a visit Mr Jones the butcher who would recommend the best that he had on offer that day, meat butchered close by, hung to perfection and the offal couldn't have been fresher. Beef and pork sausages, chipolatas and faggots were made in the shop and could all be bought singly, the mince prepared in the customers view. No fancy flavours just good quality beef and pork. Then came Mr Shepherd the fruit and vegetable man with his horse and cart. Fresh daily and weighed on large brass scales at the door, the vegetables were emptied straight from the brass scale pan into the housewives magical apron, better than any bag and able to carry everything. The bonus from these doorstep deliveries was the horse pooh collected with an old tin shovel to use in the garden on the vegetable crop. All of these people readily gave their advice the plainest of food tasted wonderful and seemed to be more enjoyable, again it was fresher, often picked on the day it was used, it was only available for short periods and you looked forward to it, you never became bored by it. It all tasted earthy and distinctive and didn't need to be smothered in spices as it had a flavour of its own.

This is what made the community in those days, people spoke in the streets,gave advice freely and willingly,you entered a shop and were always greeted,.it was deemed ill-mannered if you failed to acknowledge people with a friendly greeting.

++

Thinking back the housewives during the postwar years worked tirelessly to eradicate the pests which plagued everyday lives,the era was for these unwanted interlopers a bit like a nightmare.DDT powder was liberally sprinkled on the doorsteps to kill the ants and the little red,crab like,spiders which appeared at times.Jam jars were half-filled with water and a little jam, then the lid screwed on with a hole punched in it for wasps to crawl in and drown.DDT was sprinkled in the bath for the silverfish if you were lucky enough to have a bathroom. The "piece de resistance" was the long sticky paper strips that we hung from the ceiling,ready, to ambush the unsuspecting fly who was taking a shortcut from one room to another.It can only be described as grotesque, as we watched more and more of the little pests struggling,as they died stuck fast by their legs and wings.The luckiest flying pest was the housefly who was lucky enough to die almost instantly,hit by a rolled up newspaper or what looked similar to a fish slice ....no simple aerosols in those years!

++

The windy weather brought back memories of billowing sheets,clean, crisp, white washing flapping wildly in light summer breezes or gusty winter gales,hanging about fifteen feet up on a washing line which had been hauled up to such dizzy heights by some line and pulley system.The wooden pegs holding them securely in place till it had dried,bought from the travelling gypsies that called from time to time..No washing basket in those days,it was carried in a large enamel bowl tucked under the washer woman's arm,along with the clothes peg bag!

 Once dry it was neatly folded,or hung onto a wooden clothes horse in front of the open coal fire to air.In the early 1950's the flat irons were heated on the gas ring,or sometimes on the open fire.When hot the iron was picked up with a cloth,to avoid getting burnt,a lump of beeswax rubbed across the bottom to make sure it was clean and slid easier. The ironing was done on the scullery table with an old white sheet placed on it,to protect both the clean washing and the tabletop..When finished and folded neatly it was placed either in drawers with copious mothballs or a large blanket box smelling of camphorated oil,the main problem was the clothes moths which lived on the natural fibres of wool,cotton and linen.Once artificial fibres came in in large quantities they began their demise.

 Back to school on.Monday morning saw me dressed in knee length grey socks,short grey flannel trousers,white shirt and short sleeved pullover and black highly polished shoes,at least until I got them scuffed by playing football or climbing walls. I used to walk,or more accurately skip down Leesland Road into Harcourt Road and finally into Whitworth Road.As I walked with Nana down the heavily tree lined road,the lime green new foliage,or the bare leafless branches would greet us in the relevant season.It was a pleasant walk,more of a chase,as more and more pals met up along the way,by the time we all arrived at the school gates it was quite a group..We tried to avoid Smith Street,unless we were late and had taken a shortcut,just in case Alan was there to scare us by bellowing and chasing us.Alan frightened us but he was harmless,he was autistic and our understanding of the condition almost nil.In spite of a crossing warden,it was dangerously possible to run straight out of the gate and onto the road.The school at Leesland was surrounded by black iron pointed railings,in which stood the said gate,inside the playground was three or four large horse

chestnut[conker] trees....a great asset for the extreme sports,or to us just a bit of harmless fun,as it was then just the sublime game of conkers,no Health and Safety to stunt understanding or development.
 At the gate we were handed our pull-tie shoe bags containing our plimsolls and sometimes a smuggled in weapon,maybe consisting of a hollow stalk from a plant,a perfect pea shooter, and a handful of dried peas.I remember clearly hitting Mr Bouland,one of my teachers with such a tiny projectile and clearer still the slipper across my bum a few moments later!
 Monday was savings day, the little paper saving stamp booklets with red writing were held together with a staple in which we stuck the sixpenny or one shilling savings stamps,decorated with portrait pictures of Prince Charles and Princess Anne.If we were diligent we could save until the page was full and then buy National Savings Certificates or put money into our blue Post Office Savings Bank books.Following on from the war this was meant to encourage us to save and Monday was the day the stamps were issued.

++

 Shrove Tuesday heralded the religious festival of Lent and traditionally in the 's we had pancakes,signifying the using up of less everyday foodstuffs,before"giving up " one beloved item for Lent The thin pancakes were usually served with lemon and sugar or possibly jam as we were still feeling the after affects of the war.The next day,Ash Wednesday we were made to give up a much loved item for Lent and for us kids it was quite often chocolate,still a scarce commodity, but more often sugar.We always thought this was unfair as sweet rationing had only just ended.I think that this type of action has run out now but I did manage to stop taking sugar,permanently, in my drinks of tea one year and that stayed with me all my life!!
 Although I can't say I was particularly a religious person that kind of thing at that time seemed to be the right thing to do.

++

Grandad was an absolute treasure.He was a dour man,who never learnt to drive, who walked everywhere,his long rain coat,if not worn carried over his arm,always finished off with a working mans peaked cap and black highly polished shoes..He always wore a suit and carried a silver albert chain and large pocket watch tucked into his waistcoat pocket,in the coat pocket was a long silver cigarette case and cigarette lighter which went with him everywhere.He worked at Burtons the tailors in the high street and when he had finished work headed for his pint at "The Junction" public house on the corner of Leesland Road.before he came home for dinner.In those days the pub was very limited in its beverages and the decor more akin to a horses stable than a hostelry....real "spit and sawdust".Sometimes I would wait at the door and peer in, but more often than not we waited on Nana's doorstep and ran down to greet him around the junction of Tribe Road.
A little further along on the opposite side of the road was the last remaining bombsite in Leesland Road on which grew violet michaelmas daisies.white ox eye daisies and purple veronica scattered in amongst the brambles as a silent reminder to the missing houses.
Grandad remembered this site well and to his embarrassment so did Nana,who was not inclined to let his memory slip.When,in 1941 the bomb that fell on the missing terrace exploded Grandad had foolishly lingered on his way down to the Anderson bomb shelter at the bottom of the garden of No 80 Leesland Road and he didn't arrive in time.When the "all clear" sounded Nana thought she had seen the last of him, but no not him......he was hanging by his braces from the apple tree in the tiny garden having been swept off his feet by the blast.It proved how lucky he was as tragically several lives were lost in those houses just further down.

Whenever he was reminded of the incident he would scowl and mutter to himself but a kinder or gentler man you wouldn't ever meet.

++

It was almost bedtime now and after I had returned from the cemetery with Nana I started to help her prepare for tea which was at four o'clock prompt.Cold days would see me toasting crumpets and slices of toast over an open fire using a three pronged wire toasting fork.These would arrive at the table, piled high on a plate, dripping with butter which in turn would be covered with home-made strawberry,raspberry or blackcurrant jam.
 Sunday was special so on the table would be a Victoria sponge,liberally dusted with caster sugar,joined by the all important strawberry jelly usually in the shape of a castellated mould and also released from its mould,a pink blancmange rabbit.It was indeed a "high tea" which soon after it was consumed, just as we were clearing away, was interrupted by a peal of bells from Saint Faith's Church summoning the congregation to six o'clock evensong.After the walk to the service,then listening to a sermon which we didn't completely understand, we wandered home very tired to partake of the final nightcap.Nana turned the little brown bakelite radio on with the dial on the front and drinking a cup of hot Cocoa,Horlicks or Ovaltine we listened to "Sing Something Simple" a selection of simple songs sung by the Cliff Adams Singers bringing memories back from Nanas generation.
 Goodnight and I hope you have enjoyed sharing my Sunday journey.

++

 Eaten dinner, I helped wash up and now after a wash,ugh,Nana brushed my hair,and we were ready to go.Sunday afternoon may have been peculiar to my family,but almost certainly not,so with Nana dressed in her Sunday best, a long blue coat and straw hat held in place with the obligatory hatpin we sallied forth across the road to Shepherds the florist Strangely we were carrying a small grey bag containing a pair of what looked like sheep shears,a bottle of brown liquid "Sangral"grass fertiliser,scissors and a galvanised watering can.

Having purchased a bunch of flowers from Mrs Sands florists shop, we walked up Leesland Road with me skipping up and down on the little walls which were about three bricks high, accompanied by Nana shouting "you'll fall off"...and no doubt on occasions I did.

Passing 'The Foresters Arms" public house we wandered down to Anns Hill Old cemetery.Through the gates past the groundsmans office,a swift visit to see the fish in the round ornamental pond,hiding amongst the water lily pads,then along one of the wide gravel pathways that led to the back of the less visited burial ground.We placed flowers on a small child's grave and made sure it was tidy.Nana used to talk as she tended it, remembering my uncle Phil who had died from consumption in 1912.

All tidy we then went out of the gates,crossed the road and entered the new cemetery,where just inside we visited two graves,those of my mum and grandad.My task was to remove the dead flowers to a wire waste bin and collect water from a standpipe...hence the watering can.The marble stones were wiped clean,fresh water and flowers put in the vases and the shears used to clip the grass on the grave.A new can of water had a cap of"Sangral"added,the rose put on the watering can and the grass watered with the fertilizer to keep it green.The final check on the lead letters,forming the inscription, on the grave for damage and then the long walk back.

Such was my Nanas dedication that this took place even if the rain was pouring out of the sky.The rewards were great however and for her she was satisfied that she had done her duty.

++

   Sundays when I was a kids was a "day of rest',it was designated the day of rest,the majority of the population were practising Christians,devout in their beliefs.There was no playing outside,you were expected to be quiet,no shops were,open except for florists near the cemetery at Anns Hill,or near to hospitals,in fact it was very like a ghost town it was so quiet.The first job as with everyday was to feed the chickens at the bottom of the garden and collect any eggs.After breakfast of cereal,limited by very little variety,sometimes one of the eggs I had collected,but either way at ten minutes to eight the church bells at Saint Faith's Church would signal eight o'clock communion. Nana was a pious religious lady who would attend every week and then return to prepare Sunday dinner for the family,always promptly served at midday.
Sunday dinner,every week, was a gastronomic delight of roast meat and seasonal vegetables,wherever possible grown on the family allotment,maybe we would have Yorkshire pudding, but only if we had beef,and roast potatoes.Potatoes roasted,with the joint in the meat tray so appetising, flavoured with the meat juices and always crisp.The gravy was made in the same meat tray which had had the dripping poured off into a jug,a spoon or two of Bisto,water added, and then brought to the boil on top of the gas stove.
   Pudding,we weren't posh enough for desert, consisted of fruit pie made in an enamel dish, the pastry top liberally sprinkled with caster sugar,the little pie funnel sticking out the top and creamy homemade custard where we vied to get the custard skin!
   Dinner over,washing up done and after a 'nap' the Sunday afternoon routine would begin.
++

   Austerity was not a word being bandied around wantonly but few really comprehend true austerity.In the years of the post war era we had austerity in abundance but due to experience we survived with "make do and mend" austerity to us just normal life. Credit was alien, except maybe the corner shop that would let you pay at the end of the week, and if you didn't have the money you went without. Nana would have tins, recycled from various sources but one favourite was the tall silver NHS baby milk powder and these would contain myriads of treasures that could be re-used to save money. Hours could be whiled away with a button tin on a wet day in the school holidays.

Other tins contained hooks, eyes, elastic. tape, pins, needles plus much more and the sewing box contained apart from darning wool, a mushroom, bodkins, cotton reels and other repair necessities,
It may not have been "cool" but we went to school clothed. I went to school with leather patches on the elbows of my jumper, cardboard in my shoes, shoelaces repaired with knots, darns in my socks, and very often second hand clothes, but I was happy and Nana was not in debt and "made ends meet". We may not have been dressed in the latest fashion, we may have dressed oddly, but we were clean, warm and thankful... what went wrong.

++

Maybe it was the sign of the times but in the 1950's the one person I don't remember much about was the postman. I clearly remember him at Christmas, when he had so much mail to deliver that his round was supplemented by hoards of "temporary" postman who turned up certainly sometimes three times a day and for the last two weekends before Christmas delivered on Sundays. In those days Christmas preparations didn't start much more than two weeks before Christmas Day. You could feel the excitement building to a crescendo, unlike today's watered down version starting in AUGUST

The rest of the year I remember little of the post, except the few cards on my birthday,very few cards were handed to the recipient but even your parents posted them.There seemed to be a sense of excitement and anticipation receiving it through the letterbox..Maybe it was that events were less commercial..many utility bills were paid at the doorstep,rates were paid at the town hall,the gasman collected at the doorstep,the rent man too.Postal use was predominantly for business,relatives writing from afar,and postcards from people on holidays and guess what…people talked to each other more.

++

  I sat here thinking about my Nana's and other people's fear of thunder,their knowledge of storms and lightning conductors was limited,but they new of the damage a lightning strike could cause.My thoughts ran to the cupboard under the stairs and what apart from brooms and a huge brown painted tin "blanket box"...not to be forgotten from the constant smell of camphor and mothballs which came from it,was actually in it.What kept me company when Iwas thrust in it to shelter from the lightning.Well in the corner painted in battleship grey and with a dial on the front reminiscent of a tin opener,the bit you turn, was the gas meter.Shillings,bobs, were feed to it when it was hungry giving a constant supply of gas..God help you if the box filled up before the gasman came as you would have to make a journey to town to arrange a special collection.
  How often the gas man came I can't remember but he must have been a power lifter as he emptied the meter into his bag and after a few visits along the road it must have been very heavy. He would count the money and then give some back and it would go straight back in the meter.What it was for I have no idea.
  I often wondered where the money went until one day I saw him paying money in at Whitworth Road Post Office.

That cupboard,must have"saved my life" numerous times.Hidden in its confines whilst Nana risked her own,covering the mirror,hiding the knives and cutlery before joining me in the dark.It was just fortunate that it was only on one occasion that a storm occurred during dinner time and dinner was abandoned due to lack of knife and fork!

++

Leesland Road up to Oxford Road was quite a long walk but Nana did it every day come rain or shine.She would pick me up in the morning so Dad could go to work and return me in the evening as well as providing meals..It was a difficult time, Mum was seriously ill and eventually passed away which is how the situation had arisen but Nana was a little lady and the pushchair was heavy.
 The pale blue pram with white tyres was a bulky piece of equipment and not easily manouvreable..As I became a little older I would ride a large maroon and cream tricycle with a large carrying box on the back which was opened with a large chrome handle,Nana almost running to keep up with me.When we arrived home at Oxford Road we used to call Grandad from the allotment where he cultivated various"seasonal veg",none of this you can have anything all year,if it wasn't the correct season then you could not have it.
 The veg was fresher, tastier,healthier and you looked forward to when it was available next time,you would wait a whole year to have strawberries and the season was short. I remember in the mid to late 50's asking what the pile of rag was in the allotment shed and Grandad took it out and laid it on the ground.It turned out to be the remains of a WW2 silk parachute canopy that he had kept after it appeared on the allotment after an air raid one night and he used it to cover the allotment if it was going to be a frosty night.As I became older then the season was made longer by foreign imports of vegetables which Mr

Shepherd would sell from his horse and cart,gradually making the seasonal qualities less discernible.

++

Nothing was wasted and even the dust which accumulated at the bottom of the coal shed was put to good use.A small bag of cement was purchased from the hardware shop in Whitworth Road and placed in the pushchair to carry home,hopefully on a day when my legs were not too tired.Once home the coal dust and cement was mixed in equal quantities with water before being formed in to "briquettes to be burnt on the house fire.Using recycled corn flake packets cut down to roughly the size of a house brick the thick liquid was poured in and left in the sun to dry,before being stored in the coal shed,ready to augment the winter fuel supply.

++

Every day the front doorstep was scrubbed,hands on knees,sleeves rolled up armed with a bristle hand brush and a bar of red carbolic soap the path was vigorously scrubbed till it gleamed.It was then wiped of with a dry cloth,before being left to dry completely in the wind and sun.Having done that attention was turned to the heavy brass knocker and letterbox,some houses also had a large brass door knob,all of which were polished till they gleamed.At last the entrance to the little terraced house was ready to greet any visitors that might arrive that day. and then the door was ready to meet its visitors for the day.The coalman came through that door,for some reason I think it was a Mr Blundell, and he would carry the coal through the house to the coal shed in the back garden..Meanwhile if his horse,stood with the cart, in the road outside,decided to deposit a gift then the entire female population of the road would descend in their head scarfs and pinnies armed with zinc bucket and tin shovels to collect it for the garden.

++

 Money being short,every penny counted so myself and my friends tended to entertain ourselves as it was the cheapest option, especially if you were two old age pensioners on a limited income,there was little to spare and having a mischievous grandson didn't help.At the back of the terrace houses were small backyards which the living room window looked out onto,next to the door to the scullery[kitchen].In the backyard was a perforated zinc meat safe,attached to the wall,an outside loo,in most cases a smelly drain,which was scrubbed with bleach daily,plus a tin bath which hung on the wall.This left just enough room to play with a tennis ball.The sash window to the living room would be open about six inches and my entertainment was to kick the tennis ball against the wall beneath the window,what appeared to be a harmless act, but in fact I was trying to get it through the gap of the open window.Why you may ask.Well,inside the living room,on the opposite side to the window,Grandad would sit in his old armchair,with a bottle of stout and rollup cigarette,quietly reading the daily news paper,so it caused chaos,if I had aimed it accurately, when the ball landed .Shouts emanated of "you little b******r'',followed by Nana shouting "leave the boy alone he's not doing any harm"....I.think the marital accord was not in agreement there!
 Needless to say one day I missed the gap and broke the window and that ended the fun, however that was to lead to another adventure which proved to cause even more problems.

++

Russian cake had absolutely no connection with Russia at all.When the delivery driver arrived with his daily delivery to the little bakery,he collected any stale cake left from the day before.He would do this every day,taking it back to the bakery where all the different stale cake was mixed together, before pouring a rum flavoured syrup over it to moisten it, then placing the mixture between two sponge layers,returning it to the shop the following day as Russian cake which was sold in slices

++

Thursday was pension day, the first port of call being at the bottom of Leesland Road around the corner at The Junction public house and into the post office.Money securely collected I would accompany Nana down to the Co-op shop opposite The Gipsy Queen to pay for the groceries which had been delivered on the previous Tuesday.Having settled the bill the little green book was handed into the cashier containing the following weeks order.Crossing the road to the bus stop outside Central School we boarded a number seven Provincial bus,alighting at the Gosport Library,almost opposite the Ritz cinema. This day followed the same pattern every week unless one of us was ill or I was at school.If we were ill a visit to Dr Raperport would be the order of the day.Dr Raperport's surgery was just along from the library. If the doctors services were not needed we would walk down the road at the side of the library and into North Street,the normal routine was to go to Murphys,a general stores at the corner of Mumby Road,then along to Arnetts,the fishmongers in North Cross Street, If they didn't have the required fish we would then visit Hoopers,another fishmonger and poulterer on the corner of the High Street and South Street.From there it was on into Liptons or the Maypole to choose and buy tea or cheese.The next part of the journey was my favourite as I ran down to

the corner of Bemisters Lane and waved to grandad who would be doing his little cleaning job in Burtons the tailors.Down Bemisters Lane,which ran alongside the tailors to Guntons the florist,why I didn't know because we never seemed to purchase anything although the shop was well stocked. The next two stops were Woolworths,known as the sixpenny shop that sold virtually everything, and Littlewoods,to buy bacon.To me the point of the day was a visit to Greens, or Smith and Vospers both small bakers and cake shops.No real fancy cakes just everyday types,my favourite being a slice of Russian Cake or Coconut Madeleines, as a very special treat it might be the day for a cream cake. Down to the ferry bus station .onto the number seven bus,getting off when we arrived at the stop at the top of Whitworth Road.Into Mr Jones's the butchers for the week's meat order,and no fridges,some we took with us,the rest delivered by a young man on a push bicycle during the week,some picked up on Saturday. Dyers Dairy for some eggs and butter,pay the paper bill at the little newsagent
then up Leesland Road to home and patiently wait till tea time to have my cake .It was a long day for a seven year old in 1956,but I could die for that simple routine again.

++

 Although Mum died when I was four, my real first lasting experience of family loss came when Grandad died in 1958 Funerals were very different in those years,much more sombre,much more solemn and respectful.Neighbours houses drew their curtains when somebody died and the coffin would return home normally to rest in the "parlour" the night before the burial.Friends and neighbours would come and pay their respects and the family would have a candlelight vigil at the coffin as a mark of respect.I remember Grandad's coffin being taken into the front room and me saying I was scared to my Nana.She took me into the room,saying there is nothing to be frightened of and Grandad has gone to heaven,she said you don't need to see the body but just see what you wish.My memory was of the luxurious silk or satin lining of the casket and how highly polished the oak wood of the casket was.The undertakers were Croslands,from Forton Road,they came on the morning of the funeral to screw the lid down on the coffin after everyone had said a last goodbye.After the service at St Faith's Church the cortege proceeded up Leesland Road,passing number 80 for the last time on its way to Ann's Hill Cemetery,the leading mourner walking in front of the hearse to the cemetery and on to the internment.It was so respectful and serene.

++

Number 80 Leesland Road was a two up two down,Victorian terrace property with a small scullery and gas lighting downstairs and candles complete with enamel sticks for upstairs,there was no electric lighting. A "gazunder"was under the bed to avoid going out to the well equipped outside loo at night,well equipped enough to have no lights.a gap under the door to invite all the creepy crawlies in to watch your daily ablutions and if your luck was really in the Izal and Bronco,both similar to grade two sandpaper had run out so you could have to use cut squares of newspaper threaded on to a length of knotted string.What a great job that was to give the kids one rainy afternoon.
Was I the only one to experience such child cruelty!

++

Tuesday was generally the day that groceries arrived from the Co-op stores,delivered by a tall balding gentleman in a red and gold sign written electric vehicle.The entire process had normally started on the previous Thursday.On Thursday Nana would go to Whitworth Road

P.O and get her pension book stamped after which they gave her the money.She then walked down to the Co-op on the corner of the road opposite the old Central School.when there she paid for the previous week's groceries at a little glass enclosed desk.She handed in the book,took her money and kept the book which had the next Tuesday's order written by Nana.The front door had been left "on the jar" and the driver pushed it open carried in a small cardboard box through to the scullery calling out as he entered.It was so trusting as sometimes you weren't even in the house.If something was missing from the order you would tell them the next week and they would replace it with no question!! That box was full of paper packets of various staple goods but one that fascinated me was the salt.This was delivered in a block about the size of a house brick which Nana ground down used the carving knife to turn it into grains for the salt jar!

++

Well there we are,everyday matters which have changed so very much.Some of you will have similar memories and some of you will find it hard to believe that there was a time when people lived like this.I assure you that they did but most important is that these times were enjoyed by many of your own relatives.Take time,write down,or at least tell your family your memories,otherwise there will be a time when you are gone and those invaluable memories are gone too…and no way to get them back!

++